THERE IS A DIFFERENCE

ABOUT THE AUTHORS:

John P. Fieg, a program chairman at the Washington International Center, was formerly editor of *International Exchange News*, the Center's quarterly publication. After graduating from the University of Notre Dame and receiving a master's degree in journalism from Northwestern University, Mr. Fieg spent two years in Thailand as a Peace Corps volunteer. He recently earned a law degree from George Washington University.

John G. Blair is currently editor of the Washington International Center's quarterly publication, the *International Exchange News*. He received an undergraduate degree and a master's degree in Latin American political studies from Kent State University. Mr. Blair spent two years in Chile as a Peace Corps volunteer.

Cover design by Kerry L. Witmer

THERE *IS* A DIFFERENCE

12 Intercultural Perspectives

John P. Fieg

and

John G. Blair

Meridian House International
Washington, D.C.

Library of Congress Cataloging in Publication Data

Fieg, John P   1941–
   There *Is* a difference.

  1. United States–Foreign opinion. 2. National
characteristics. I. Blair, John G., 1942–   joint
author. II. Meridian House International. III. Title.
E169.12.F48   309.1'04'7   75–5939

Printed by Fontana Lithograph, Inc.

To the more than 110,000 international visitors from nearly 150 nations and territories who have participated in the programs of the Washington International Center since its establishment in 1950.

PREFACE

The need to be aware of, to identify and to accept the differences in thought patterns, life styles, and goals of peoples from around the world has been an area of increasing concern to volunteers and staff of the Washington International Center. On the recommendation of the volunteer-staff committee planning the Center's observance of its 25th anniversary, we decided to share our experiences through this book in the belief that they might prove interesting and helpful to a wider audience, particularly to those working with international visitors.

Many individuals have contributed to the preparation and production of this publication — far too many to record here. However, we must extend our special thanks to the many international visitors in Washington who gave so freely of their time and thoughts during interviews: to Dr. Peter F. Krogh, dean of Georgetown University's School of Foreign Service and chairman of Meridian House International's Trustees Committee on the Washington International Center, for his support and guidance; to Mrs. Frances B. Sayre, Sr., former chairman of WIC volunteers, whose generous contribution helped underwrite our publication costs; to WIC volunteer, Mrs. Alan C. Newburger for her competent advice and willing assistance; and finally to our staff author/editors, John P. Fieg and John G. Blair whose perception and creativity was not diminished by the pressures to meet deadlines.

James A. Coughlin
Executive Director

March 13, 1975

CONTENTS

PREFACE   vii

INTRODUCTION   1

1. BRAZIL   8
    John P. Fieg

2. INDIA   12
    John P. Fieg

3. JAPAN   18
    John P. Fieg

4. KENYA   27
    John P. Fieg

5. TURKEY   33
    John P. Fieg

6. COLOMBIA   41
    John P. Fieg

7. INDONESIA   49
    John P. Fieg

8. ETHIOPIA   58
    John P. Fieg

9. JAMAICA   68
    John P. Fieg

10. IRAN   78
    John G. Blair

11. EGYPT   88
    John P. Fieg

12. NIGERIA   99
    John G. Blair

PERSPECTIVES   109

INTRODUCTION

A Vietnamese visitor to Washington, D.C. ordered a turkey dinner and wanted to indicate to the waitress that he preferred light meat. Unfortunately this term was not part of his working vocabulary, so he quickly thought of a nonverbal indicator: he pointed to his chest. The waitress brought him a glass of milk. Clearly a problem in intercultural communication.

Having arrived in the United States the day before, an Afghan came to the Washington International Center cafeteria for his first breakfast in this country. He sat down at one of the tables, obviously expecting someone to take his order. The Center's director explained to him that this was a "self-service" arrangement and pointed the way to the start of the line. Ten minutes later the startled director found the man behind the serving counter about ready to crack open an egg and prepare his own breakfast. He had taken the director's words literally.

An Indonesian was quite satisfied with the apartment he had rented but was perplexed when he returned from school the first day, only to notice the sign at the entrance to his block: "Do Not Enter." "How can I get home when entry is not allowed?" he wondered. Even a simple traffic sign can pose problems in communication for one not accustomed to the new cultural environment.

Intercultural communication obviously has its lighter moments; but it has a serious side too. There is a constant temptation to label what is different about another culture as wrong or even immoral. Take individualism for example. To an American it has the positive connotation of personal liberty; to an African, however, individualism may indicate loneliness or disharmony. An American parent will try to give his children separate bedrooms to ensure their privacy. This is taken by a visitor from Bangladesh as proof positive that American parents do not love their children; if they did, they would obviously sleep together in the same room.

At the Washington International Center we have the unusual and highly interesting challenge of trying to make understandable to visitors from nearly 150 countries and territories the complexities of the ever-changing American society they are about to enter. To borrow from space age terminology, we try to cushion their entry into the United States and at the same time to serve as a launch pad for their impending journey out into an alien cultural milieu.

We thus want to extend a warm — but not protective — welcome. We want to help, but not to patronize. Our dual functions of greeting and orienting can come into conflict, for to the extent that our program engenders dependence, it is detrimental to one who must acquire a certain measure of self-reliance during his sojourn in the United States. At the same time we must be aware of the trite-but-true saying that first impressions are lasting and thus try to make each visitor feel immediately at home.

The Washington International Center (WIC) was established in 1950 by the American Council on Education, a private association of American colleges and universities. WIC is today administered by Meridian House International, a nonprofit cultural and educational organization.

Ideally a visitor will take part in the WIC program just after he arrives in the country and will, if possible, spend a full week at the Center. Through a series of seminars, educational tours, and social functions he will hopefully have the chance to gain a deeper understanding of the United States and its people in a relaxed, congenial atmosphere.

Volunteers play an important part in the overall Center program. They meet visitors at the airport, escort them on tours of Capitol Hill and historic Washington, and arrange dinners with American families. They also take visitors to cultural and athletic events and answer questions about such practical matters as shopping and banking. Meeting volunteers gives visitors a chance to see how abstract seminar comments concerning American behavior are reflected in the day-to-day interaction of individual Americans.

Government leaders, professional people, students, and technicians — many of them sponsored by the Agency for International Development (AID) or the United Nations — comprise the majority of the Center's clientele. They are in the United States for advanced academic or technical training in such fields as public administration, education, agriculture, public health, community development, and economics. Most come from

East and South Asia, Africa, and Latin America.

As we look back over our 25-year history, we see that the Center has in some ways been a microcosm of American society. In its infancy in the early 1950's, the Center tended to project (as did American society in general) the persistent puritan notion of America as the utopian "City on the Hill." To know us was to want to emulate us. If only visitors from abroad had the chance to observe how wonderful we really were, they would race back to rebuild their tradition-laden homelands in the image of the American colossus.

The information flow was one way. We tended to *tell* visitors what we thought they should know rather than share ideas with them and thereby really communicate. Cultural differences didn't exist, for if you scratched the skin of an American, a Japanese, and a Ghanaian, weren't they all esentially the same? And, being reasonable people, wouldn't foreign visitors naturally pattern themselves after our free, prosperous, democratic society?

Following this initial stage of near-missionary zeal, we embarked on a more balanced approach in which divergent viewpoints were encouraged and a more sophisticated look was taken at American institutions. But the emphasis was still on information, without enough attention as to how such knowledge would actually help someone adjust to life in American society.

We have now learned that man does not live by facts alone. Rather there must be a constant attempt to relate various aspects of American life to the visitor's own cultural background. How can we explain the American's concern over an "invasion of privacy" to someone whose language (Turkish, Amharic, Japanese, Arabic) does not have an exact equivalent of "privacy"? Can we say that Americans are emotionally expressive or reserved until we know the cultural perspective? Brazilians, for example, might find us cold and unemotional, whereas Southeast Asians would view us as choleric and vibrant.

As we have modified our program, we have attempted to learn more about which aspects of American life are particularly troublesome to visitors from different parts of the world. We have tried to understand how an African's insight into our culture might differ significantly from an Asian's, how an Arab's adjustment might vary from a Latin's.

In entering our young adulthood we feel that we have, like American society in general, matured to the extent that we can now engage in a true sharing and exchange of ideas with international visitors. Not the least benefit of this reciprocal relationship is the chance for individual visitors to learn more about the customs and cultures of one another, for no longer are they compelled to sit silently and absorb perhaps more then they ever wanted to know about the geological structure of the Rocky Mountains or the War of 1812.

When we began to place greater emphasis on the visitor's adjustment and accommodation to our society, the need to link the theory and practice of intercultural communication became readily apparent. How does one discuss cultural differences with a group as heterogeneous in terms of customs, patterns of thinking, and English ability as a typical weekly group at the International Center?

We had to refine and simplify anthropological abstractions and try to identify those areas of American life which are most difficult for visitors from different cultures to understand. We then had to discover how to introduce these cultural variants in a coherent, comparative manner so as to give the visitors the chance to discuss these usually novel concepts while first impressions were fresh in mind.

A way should be found to somehow systematize cultural differences and relate them directly to the American society the visitors would soon encounter. Many excellent anthropological works provide an insight into the patterns of culture in other societies, but relatively few seem to take a directly contrastive approach to cultural differences, that is to analyze a given aspect of one culture in relation to another. Yet it was exactly this comparative approach that we needed if we were to set our discussions of cultural differences in a context that would be comprehensible to such a diverse group.

It was then that we hit on the idea of doing the series of articles which forms the heart of this book. Each of the succeeding 12 chapters appeared originally in our quarterly publication, *International Exchange News,* which is sent to all former participants in the WIC program. In concentrating on one country per quarter, we tried to find out the most crucial cultural differences between that country and the United States and to give examples of how these fundamental variances manifest themselves in the everyday interaction between Americans and those from the featured country.

In interviewing people from a given country, we tried purposely to include as wide a range as possible in terms of age, occupation, social status, and length of time in the U.S. Anonymity of the respondents was assured in order to encourage the most frank, accurate analysis. We interviewed men and women, students and professors, interpreters and economists, embassy personnel and permanent residents. One interview followed a five-course Indonesian dinner; another was held in a Washington hotel at 1 a.m. – the only free time of a busy Japanese executive.

Often a theoretical concept would be strikingly particularized in a casual question and comment. We have read, for example, that the achievement-oriented American tends to emphasize "doing" and being highly active, whereas in some other societies more importance is attached to what a person *is* than what he *does.*

This textbook abstraction was brought forcefully to life when we asked an Indonesian woman who had just returned from a year in Bali, "What were you *doing* there?" "Just living," she replied, thereby causing us to take a new look at the cultural perspective embodied in our matter-of-fact question.

Usually the interview would begin with a general question about what aspects of American society had seemed most unusual or were most difficult to understand or adjust to in terms of the interviewee's own culture and customs. This served to set his focus on the most crucial areas of misunderstanding between the two cultures and gave us a clue as to what topics to pursue in this discussion and succeeding interviews.

We would then move to more specific areas, such as interpersonal relations, family patterns, use of time and space, and attitudes toward individualism, egalitarianism, and emotional expressiveness. Many questions related to particular aspects of a given culture that were familiar to (but often misunderstood by) those outside the culture, such as Islam in Egypt, polygyny in Kenya, or lifetime employment with the same company in Japan.

Most of those interviewed had been in the United States for at least one year, and some had lived here considerably longer. The few attempts to interview recent arrivals were not wholly satisfactory, for it seems that in order to compare fundamental cultural patterns of two societies, one must live long enough in the alien environment to see clearly the real areas of difference. Without this period of exposure to the new society, the interviewee tended to highlight superficial differences and to downplay the deep-seated cultural variations which affect behavior in the two societies.

Interviews were also conducted with Americans who had lived in the featured country in order to learn more about what aspects of that culture were most difficult for Americans to adjust to. These comments enabled us to pass on to participants in our orientation program some of the difficulties Americans had had in adjusting to life in their countries. Armed with an awareness of these fundamental differences, an individual who took part in our program would hopefully be better able to see how he might have to modify his conduct in certain instances in order not to alienate Americans while in the U.S.

Since obviously no two interviews proceeded in exactly the same way, it is difficult to convey a sense of the introspective force and the sheer intellectual energy expended in trying to arrive at a comprehensible answer to a purposely difficult question. Some of those interviewed seemed to sense at once the types of comparisons we were trying to make; others became aware more slowly during the course of the interview. Virtually all seemed to appreciate the challenge of trying to express analytically — and often for the first time — some of their thoughts and theories about cultural differences.

The Biblical message that it is easier to see the splinter in another's eye than the beam in one's own was clearly borne out in the response to a two-part question concerning things Americans did that would be considered rude or impolite in their societies and conversely, behavior which in their societies would be acceptable but that Americans would consider improper.

Nearly everyone interviewed could quite readily list several examples of American behavior that would be offensive in terms of his culture, but almost to a man (or woman) they had trouble citing aspects of their conduct that Americans would frown on. Follow-up questions could almost always elicit some manifestations of their behavior that caused problems for Americans, but the important point to note is that these examples often had to be called to their attention, whereas responses concerning the "peculiarities" of American conduct needed no such triggering mechanism.

Preferences for one's own cultural patterns would sometimes interfere with an objective appraisal of the two societies, and thus a value judgment would color an otherwise accurate description of differences in behavior. A clear understanding of the particular difference was present, but this was not accompanied by a deeper awareness of the underlying cultural patterns in the two societies which had led to the difference.

Generally, however, those interviewed were able to escape from the shell of ethnocentrism and analyze the cultural differences with considerable detachment, insight, and skill. In fact, some saw the differences so clearly that it distressed them when fellow countrymen or Americans would criticize — rather than try to understand — one another's culture. A Japanese businessman confessed that in one sense it was now more difficult for him to live in either the U.S. or Japan, for he caught himself being constantly impatient with those in both societies who failed to comprehend the other because they had not shared his experiences on both sides of the cultural divide.

Our attempts to compress the values, assumptions, and cultural patterns of complex societies into a series of short sketches naturally lead to generalization. Yet in describing the most fundamental patterns of thinking and culture, one must generalize if there is to be any meaningful basis of comparison. Not everyone in the United States is imbued with a strong sense of egalitarianism; yet the overall tendency or dominant thrust is in this direction. This generality may not be clearly seen, however, until the United States is compared with a society whose structure is predominantly hierarchical.

Despite the diverse backgrounds of those interviewed from a particular country, there was a striking similarity in their comments concerning the most pronounced differences between their society and the U.S. This unanimity was at first surprising, but as the interviews progressed it became clear that it was indeed possible for perceptive observers to isolate and agree to certain key cultural characteristics. Where sharp differences arose, however, we made every effort to include both sides in our article.

We offer this collection of country stories not as a definitive statement but rather as an attempt to bring into sharper focus some of the day-to-day specifics of intercultural communication — hopefully in a small way to bridge the gap between the intercultural theoretician and the layman. Only if some awareness of cultural differences is developed beyond the realm of the anthropologist or communications specialist can "international understanding" ever become more than a much mentioned cliche. We take, then, a tentative first step in a global journey which clearly has many thousands of miles to go.

1

BRAZIL

When a Brazilian bids *adeus* (farewell) to his homeland to embark on his journey to the U.S.A., he takes along with him a puzzling mix of positive and negative stereotypes about the country and the people he is going to visit.

He expects to find the "Coca-Cola Culture" — a paradise in terms of consumer goods but a populace somewhat lacking in culture and sophistication. He has great regard for such technological exploits as putting a man on the moon but has been forewarned that Americans are naive ("like big boys" in the words of one Brazilian) and overserious.

He may also be aware of some of the stereotypes that Americans have of Brazilians: a warmhearted, vivacious people with an enviable, easygoing life style but who seem to take few things seriously.

Thus the Brazilian sees the American as a somber follower of former President Calvin Coolidge's stern doctrine that "the business of America is business." The American, for his part, cannot understand how the Brazilian can dance the samba into the night and cheerfully forget tomorrow's labors.

Part of this difference in outlook can be traced to the ways in which children are raised in the two societies. The American child has impressed on him a clearer notion of what is good and what is bad; he definitely knows what he is not supposed to do if he is to avoid future problems. To a Brazilian parent, things are not that clear-cut.

"We will not say that a thing is 'right' or 'wrong,' " one Brazilian said. "We don't measure and evaluate everything the way you (Americans) do."

Because an American has been trained to look for "wrongs," he cannot understand why Brazilians do not share his crusader's zeal to combat what he views as society's problems. The Brazilian, raised to accept rather than struggle, wonders what the turmoil is all about.

The rhythm of family life differs greatly in the two societies. The Brazilian mother stays at home during the day, and even families below average economically will have servants.

"I had to adjust to a different sort of discipline," said one Brazilian exchange student who spent some time with an American family. "I had to make my own bed and get my own food from the refrigerator. I was also surprised to find out that many students here stay after school for band, football practice, or club meetings. In Brazil, school is a place to go away from when classes end.

"Even though each family member went about his own business during the day, they seemed to me to be close-knit," he added. Yet other Brazilians see a lack of solidarity in the American family because of the separate existence for much of the day.

The recently arrived Brazilian is surprised to see young American students working in supermarkets or gas stations, for manual labor is looked down on in Brazil.

"It doesn't ennoble you. A Brazilian student wouldn't consider it. He might collect and sell stamps or write, but only the very poor would work with their hands," one Brazilian said.

And only women would work in the kitchen. Brazilian males are astonished to see American men helping with the cooking. As one put it, "I wouldn't touch that thing (cooking)."

Brazilians are generally more conscious than Americans of their origins and are more interested in tracing their lineage. Proud indeed is the Brazilian who can boast of a baron in his background.

Unlike the American who turned his back on Europe and was proud to be a citizen of the "New World," the Brazilian has always turned more towards Europe as a cultural and intellectual model. In fact the very word "Brazilian" in Portuguese (*Brasileiro*) means literally "one who works in Brazil." The original connotation, then, was that the *Brasileiro* was in Brazil to work but not to stay.

Because tradition and family ties are so important in Brazil, social behavior is more predictable than in the U.S. Americans tend to deny an external cause of their behavior; one should be "spontaneous," "creative," "innovative." Whereas the Brazilian has many cues from family background and traditional mores to help him establish the proper relationship with another, the American makes a point of trying not to predetermine a person's position in a group.

And since the Brazilian's world is more ordered and predictable, he cannot understand why the American must constantly look for reactions from others to insure himself that his individualistic behavior is having the desired effect.

This difference in outlook is reflected in the Brazilian's view of the seminar format, so popular in American universities. He is uncomfortable when he is expected to question and challenge the professor, for he is accustomed to waiting until the lecture is over before discussing an unclear point.

"Having a class with the teacher as an equal is not easy for us," one Brazilian said.

But Brazilians do debate — often and profoundly. However, they prefer a more informal setting, be it the living room or soccer stadium, rather than the classroom.

Perhaps nowhere are Brazilian and American attitudes more sharply contrasted than at party time. The American custom of setting a closing time — either formally on the invitation or informally through a series of hints or yawns — is incomprehensible to the Brazilian mind.

"If we are having a good time, we will stay all night," one Brazilian said. "If not, we'll leave right away."

Social anthropologists have analyzed this difference in terms of the importance of the "occasion" in Brazil as opposed to the premium on "convenience" in the U.S.

The American hostess will innocently offend when she offers a Brazilian a plate of hors d'oeuvres saying, "Why don't you eat these; we have only three left." The hostess does not want to be inconvenienced by having to store the leftovers. To the Brazilian, convenience should not enter into the picture. The question should be whether or not you enjoy the food.

The newly arrived Brazilian is surprised to learn that many Americans with high incomes live in the suburbs, for the Portuguese equivalent of "suburb" (*arrabalde*) connotes an unsophisticated, impoverished place to live. Stranger still is the sense of community or "community spirit" which prevails in towns and villages throughout the U.S., for such a concept is for the most part absent in Brazil.

Another unusual aspect of American life as seen through Brazilian eyes is the essential sameness of life style throughout the country. One Brazilian attributes this homogeneity to the economic integration of all parts of the U.S. "Canned soup, orange juice, and bus tokens from coast to coast," he said.

Diversity rules in Brazil. Patterns of consumption and indeed life style are regional rather than national. The tropical Amazon region supports an incredible variety of animal and plant life; there are over 1,000 types of wood alone.

The people of the North depend on the earth to earn their livelihood; they are at home with nature. Generally more rugged and hardworking than the peoples of other areas, the northerners are also more shy and softspoken. The southerners are healthier, wealthier, and more in contact with the outside world.

And then there is Rio! "Life is bright and beautiful in Rio de Janeiro — beautiful beaches, beautiful women," said one Brazilian, as he thought back to the coaxing Copacabanna beach. "The ideal there is to work as little as possible."

This leaves plenty of time for romantic escapades, and the art of pursuit has been developed to perfection in Brazil. "It's a real sport, especially in Rio," one Brazilian said.

The Brazilian is thus perplexed by what he considers American reserve. "No one holds hands; not even the children," complained one. Another was disheartened by "the lack of response from the girls" when he tried to transfer Brazilian rules of romance to the American arena.

"There are very few things in life that are really serious," said one Brazilian philosophically. And Rudyard Kipling may well have had an unconscious yearning for Brazil when he wrote: "More men are killed by overwork than the importance of the world justifies."

2

INDIA

Indians and Americans share a strangely ambivalent attitude about their respective countries. Both are intensely proud, to the point of stridency at times, of their country's achievements, but they harbor a similar shame for their society's shortcomings.

Perhaps it is the very size of the world's two largest democracies that makes them so open to outside comment, for all is writ so large — both the weaknesses and the wonders — that the search for any measure of objective truth about either country is a difficult one indeed.

The American is proud of the technological achievements and material advances and believes that his country has been a land of opportunity. At the same time he is ashamed that despite these accomplishments, he cannot seem satisfactorily to combat the problems of crime, racial disharmony, and environmental pollution that are straining the seams of a society in transition.

The Indian takes a similar pride in his country's rich cultural heritage — the wealth of artistic, literary, and philosophical attainments that have flown so steadily for so long. He is justifiably proud that the national unity espoused by Gandhi has been so largely achieved without a loss of the tolerance of diversity praised by Tagore. But he is plagued by the ever-present reality of poverty and is equally disturbed that the poverty problem is played up abroad, often to the exclusion of India's accomplishments.

"Most Americans seem to know about the Taj Mahal and the slums of Calcutta but little else," one Indian student said. "But when we consider the size and diversity of our population, the numerous languages and religions, and the short 24 years of our independence, we are proud that we have stuck together."

Because the stereotype of American affluence has been accentuated in India, many recent arrivals are appalled by the grim aspect of inner-city poverty in the U.S.

"As I took a cab to my university, I saw poor housing, streets covered with shattered glass, and shops shuttered with wire meshes. It was frightening," said one Indian student.

The pace of life in the U.S. is exceptionally fast, even for those who thought themselves accustomed to a rushed existence.

"I come from Bombay where we have the same cycle of run for the office — dash for home, so I was not expecting too much of a change. But life is definitely faster in the U.S.," one student said.

"To Indian eyes Americans seem to be in a perpetual hurry. Just watch the way they walk down the street. They never allow themselves the leisure to enjoy life; there are too many things to do," added another.

The American's preference for "getting down to business" immediately seems overly abrupt to the Indian, who likes to ease into a subject gradually, usually over a cup of tea or coffee.

"Just to close the door and start a film or seminar is a little disconcerting," one Indian said.

Since many Indian visitors have servants at home, the need to be immediately independent, to do many things for oneself, can be a difficult adjustment for a recent arrival.

"I felt like a fish out of water," said one Indian, who obviously missed his four servants.

This absence of servants in the U.S. can sometimes lead to misunderstandings between Indians and Americans in such service occupations as waiter, taxi driver, and bellboy. In giving what sounds like a perfectly normal (in India) order, an Indian will shock an American waiter or clerk who feels that he is being treated harshly. The waiter may rebel, offending the Indian with his sulking service.

"There is an entirely different attitude in India. A shopkeeper out to make a sale will treat his customer with the utmost deference. But an Indian cannot expect a salesperson in the U.S. to act subservient," said one Indian who has lived for some time in the United States.

If the American detects a somewhat haughty approach in the way an Indian treats a service person, the Indian also sees signs of arrogance in the American's behavior.

"The generation of young men coming to the U.S. to study now were born into a free India. They are very aware that the white man has considered himself superior to the 'colored' man — black or brown.

They are resentful if this superior attitude shows up; if they find a hint of arrogance, this puts their hackles up," said one Indian.

"If we go to a reception and see Americans talking to Australians, New Zealanders, or South Africans and ignoring us, we feel neglected. Of course Indians feel more comfortable talking to those from a similar background too. We understand this. But no one wants to be neglected," he added.

Another attribute which Indians and Americans see in one another is a tendency to be extremely precise and analytical.

"The secret of India is compartmentalization," said an American professor who has spent considerable time in India. "A society this large — with so many races, religions, and cultures — could not survive without a compartmentalized social structure."

Thus it is important for an Indian to define himself specifically in terms of his ethnic and family background, occupation, town, and state so that he can determine the proper social relationship with another.

Americans appear precise to Indians too, but in a different way.

"If I say, 'It's hot out,' an American will say, 'Yes, it's 85 degrees,' " one Indian said. "When I say to a girl, 'What a beautiful dress,' she will say, 'I bought it in New York two weeks ago.' And why are Americans so concerned about knowing the weather forecast? They watch the weatherman; they dial the weather. We'll just look at the sky. If it's cloudy, we'll take an umbrella."

Though Indians do not face the difficult language barrier that plagues many visitors to the U.S., they do have some problem understanding English — American style. A "lift" in India is an "elevator" in the U.S.; a "frock" is a "dress;" a "waterproof" is a "raincoat," and a "biscuit," a "cookie."

"Some Americans have a way of speaking that appears to us very short and brusque, but this should not be mistaken for rudeness," said one long-time Indian resident in the U.S.

Because they are accustomed to the more conservative British sartorial style and proper etiquette, Indians are often taken aback by the Americans' loud dress and casual manners — the bright colors on the men, the "hail-fellow-well-met" posture epitomized by the boisterous "Hi" and the slap on the back.

Even more surprising is the way this informality is carried into the classroom. Though youthful Indians are perhaps more critical of their teachers than in the past, seeing American students wearing sweatshirts, drinking cokes, and smoking cigarettes in the classroom is hard to reconcile with the Hindu maxim that "Next to God is the teacher."

A former teacher in India who is familiar with both educational systems gave a perceptive analysis of the difference in outlook in the two countries.

"The seeming rudeness and lack of discipline on the part of U.S. students is simply an expression of the oneness between the teacher and those taught. There is a much more intimate rapport between the two than in India, where traditionally the teacher has been placed on a pedestal and could expect pin-drop silence. In the U.S. the students' involvement gives the impression of rudeness. It's a different growth process, that's all," he said.

The respect for the teacher is only one aspect of the Indian's esteem for the elderly, which grows out of a close-knit, sentimental family relationship. Whereas Americans may view this interdependency as an unwelcome restraint on individualism, the Indian sees the American's self-sufficiency as a heartless hurdle to domestic tranquility.

"American society has lost all use for the older people. I wouldn't like to grow old in this country. It's lonely enough being old anywhere, but it's not as bad in India, where we still have a way of accepting old age," said one Indian.

Much of this acceptance comes from a view of life shaped by Hindu philosophy, which teaches that man through his folly must endure a succession of rebirths until, by conquering his desires, he reaches a transcendent state. Old age is simply one stage in the repetitive cycle of existence, a time when through good deeds and meditation a man can come nearer the godhead.

"An Indian accepts the fact that for so many years he will be a student, for so many a householder, and then grow old. At this point he will often go to a monastery to meditate on the next life. He knows that he has done his job in this one," an Indian said.

As a sign of respect, Indian youth do not use the Hindi word which translates as "he" in English when they speak of an older person. Rather they use a word closer to "they" in English, thereby elevating the position of a revered elder.

"I found it very difficult to use 'he' to refer to my father when I was learning English," one Indian youth said. "It sounded disrespectful."

But Indians do not view all aspects of American individualism as necessarily negative. One was impressed when he saw an eight-year-old American boy ordering from a menu. This assertiveness at such an early age would be unknown in India.

"Perhaps Indians are overly sentimental and attached to their relatives, while Americans are too independent. Maybe some kind of a balance should be struck between the two," said one sensitive Indian student.

Because public displays of affection have long been considered rude and licentious in India, the recent arrival is somewhat shocked by American permissiveness.

"He will be intrigued and fascinated by Western openness, but he could hardly consider this proper," said one Indian, who was himself surprised to see couples "embracing in broad daylight while the police strolled nonchalantly by."

Though the custom of dating has eased its way into the larger Indian cities and there is even discotheque dancing in downtown Delhi, the code of conduct is much stricter than in the U.S., and to "go out" with someone generally connotes a closer emotional attachment for Indian than American youths.

"A girl will usually return home by 8 p.m.; 9 p.m. is rare, and 11 p.m. is serious," said one Indian student.

What passes for pleasant conversation or mild flirtation between U.S. males and females can easily be misinterpreted by the newly arrived Indian. For a light touch or playful wink — innocent gestures among Americans — suggest moral looseness in Indian society.

The role of the Indian woman is enigmatic to Western eyes, for she seems at once subservient and liberated, tied to the home yet free to pursue a career. As an American student of India expressed it, "When an Indian woman has economic independence and education, she can take greater advantage of this than an American woman." An outstanding example is, of course, India's Prime Minister Indira Gandhi.

Yet historically the Indian woman's life has been built around home and family.

"She has been taught that her function in life is to marry and perform certain household duties. Her husband, as the family provider, is to her God incarnate. He may be a scoundrel in the eyes of the world, but in her eyes he is a god," said one Indian.

But not every Indian woman still follows the time-honored tradition of removing her husband's shoes, fixing his bath, and preparing a snack when he returns home from work.

"Now my wife only says, 'Where have you been?' after a hard day at the office," said one Indian somewhat nostalgically.

"An Indian woman will do anything for her husband and children, but she can still attain a high position in the outside world. The American woman seems to us more glamorized and people rush to open car doors for her, yet at the same time she appears more exploited," another added.

Though marriage across caste lines is easier than in the past, such a union can pose problems in families where the tug of tradition is strong.

A Brahmin (highest caste) whose daughters married below their caste explained how some of his relatives would have nothing more to do with his family.

"The caste is like a club. Members smoke from the same pipe and drink from the same water pitcher but don't allow other castes to do so. I thought of how our relatives would not allow us to drink their water, but we can't stop this shift to free choice in marriage," he said.

There appear to be striking similarities between caste barriers in India and racial discrimination in the U.S. Legally neither exists, yet socially the deeply imbedded attitudes can not be easily erased by simple edict. Perhaps it was the dual strains of action-orientation and puritanism in both peoples that made Gandhi a leader in India and a model for the civil rights movement in the U.S.

In a reflective mood, a scholarly Indian revealed what he believes is a new, somewhat bolder attitude developing among his people.

"If you see in the Indian certain qualities which may not be associated with our culture and religious philosophy, then you must bear in mind that the Indian is aware that he has emerged as someone who ought to be reckoned with," he said. "One can debate whether this is good, bad, or indifferent, but it is a fact."

3

JAPAN

Just enough similarities exist between the United States and Japan to make it tempting to try to equate the two. Both have advanced, efficient economies, share a basic belief in a work ethic, and are noted for their technological skills.

Confident of finding certain likenesses in the life styles of the two countries as well, both Americans and Japanese are often confused by the underlying differences in cultural patterns, which can suddenly shatter the spectre of similarity.

Like a traveler who can more readily adjust to *expected* differences in a remote country than unforeseen variations in a neighboring nation, the American is caught unaware by some of the cultural differences between the two peoples. One American who spent several months in Japan termed these differences "the most penetrating and alien" that she had found in Asia.

The most apparent differences involve various mannerisms considered proper in one society but peculiar in the other. Because the Japanese have a more rigorous concept of proper and improper bodily movements, they consider it rude when Americans sit with their feet on the table or cross their legs in an "unsightly" way.

"To throw something to someone — like the keys to a room — is also considered offensive; it connotes a superior person giving something away," said one Japanese, who added that only among friends would such conduct be tolerated.

The newly arrived Japanese can be somewhat disturbed by the absence of bowing among Americans, for while to Western eyes the bow may appear subservient and somewhat effeminate, the Japanese regard it as an indispensable show of politeness.

Failure to understand such a relatively simple difference can lead to "a tense situation at the personal level," according to one Japanese student.

Accustomed to noisily sipping hot tea at home, the Japanese who sips soup in a similar way in the U.S. will present an ill-mannered picture to the American.

These surface differences are only one aspect, though, of deeper and more pervasive variations in the underlying assumptions which regulate conduct in the two societies, making each appear inscrutable to the other.

Whereas Americans prize a consistent pattern of behavior and want one to be "true to his word," the Japanese determinant of proper conduct must necessarily vary from one circumstance to the next.

"In Japan and in the Orient in general, ethics is always a function of the situation. If the situation changes, we must change too — more or less automatically," said one Japanese who has had considerable contact with Japanese and American businessmen.

"The American businessman will generally want an immediate answer in contract negotiations, or at least a timetable. From the Japanese point of view, there are complications which make it impossible to make a commitment. Thus the Japanese will say, 'We will study this and see what we can do,' " he said.

Once the contract has been signed, a further complicating factor can arise.

"If the situation changes, the Japanese businessman will say, 'Even though the contract says such and such, let's change it.' To him, he's merely being flexible; the environment has changed. But the U.S. businessman will say that this is a violation of the contract. Thus there is always a clash of approach," he said.

Caution in reaching a final decision must be deeply imbedded in the Japanese mentality, for as a Japanese woman who has lived in the U.S. for many years explained: "Whenever I am asked to do something, my first reaction is to not commit myself. I want to make sure that I don't fail to keep the commitment."

If this approach seems wavering and evasive to the American, it is viewed as being sensibly flexible by the Japanese. This flexible outlook has enabled the Japanese to borrow elements from a variety of countries and cultures and fit them into the basic Japanese mosaic.

"The Japanese have been accused of being great imitators but lacking in creativity. But we not only imitate; we adapt things we borrow to our own way. There is a certain 'melting pot' aspect," one Japanese woman said.

Because the casual glance or cryptic comment can speak volumes in Japan, a Japanese visitor finds the American stress on direct, verbal communication difficult to fathom.

"When I talk to girls at home, there is always a two-level discussion; besides the surface meaning, there is the connotation," said a Japanese student. "I must tone down my speech and mannerisms and avoid certain expressions. If I say something improper, the Japanese girl will act like she hasn't heard it, whereas an American girl will react and tell you what she thinks. It's easy to tell if she is angry. But the Japanese girl will remain expressionless."

Since Americans rely on open discussion to measure another's intelligence and interest in the topic at hand, they sometimes look askance at the silent, smiling Japanese woman. Equating stillness with ignorance, the American will conclude that the Japanese woman has sacrificed intellectual development for doll-like charm. Not surprisingly, the Japanese have a different explanation.

"It is difficult for Japanese, especially the women, to enter a circle of people they don't know. They are shy and hesitant to join in. At a dinner party, the Japanese wife feels that it is not polite for her to join the conversation; this is the husband's role. Her role is to make the guest feel welcome and serve pleasing food. She is well informed about the situation but will not speak out. She just understands," a Japanese woman said.

"The movement of the eyes tells a lot," added a Japanese student.

Thus a normal American conversation will often seem overly precise and direct to a Japanese, who wants above all to avoid offending his questioner.

"When an American says, 'Did you understand?', a Japanese will not like to say, 'No, I don't understand what you're talking about.' He will just smile and try not to pursue the subject further. We don't like to make things as clear-cut as Americans do," said one Japanese man who had lived some time in the U.S.

Coming from a society where emotional restraint is the rule, the Japanese views as effusive what the American would call moderate social intercourse.

"We would never say, 'My wife is the most beautiful girl; I love her so much.' To be boastful of a private affair is very improper. Or if someone asks us, 'Do you miss your wife?', we would answer, 'No, not at all,' for to confess weakness is unmanly," said a Japanese man.

"If I speak to someone senior to me, I'm expected to humble — not honor — my wife and would use the word *gusai* which means something like 'my stupid wife.' I would refer to the senior man's wife as 'your respectful, honorable wife,' " he added, pointing out that such expressions have nothing whatever to do with his wife's intelligence or his regard for her. It is simply a polite way to address a superior. }

"If someone says to a Japanese girl, 'You look beautiful today,' she would never say, 'Thank you,' for it would show that she was accepting the compliment. She would just say, 'No,' " a Japanese woman added.

This playing down of the self for fear of being overassertive can lead to unforeseen consequences when the proper Japanese phrasing is translated directly into English.

"In Japanese we might say, 'Come to my humble house to eat my horrible food and meet my ugly wife,' " a Japanese woman said. "But one time, a Japanese girl baked a cherry pie for her American friend, apologizing for the 'horrible pie, which didn't turn out too well.' Actually the pie had turned out beautifully, but the American girl took the Japanese girl at her word. The next day the Japanese girl was shocked to find the pie she had so carefully baked in the garbage can."

Because Japanese tend to regard the *way* in which something is said or done as perhaps more important than the word or deed itself, they generally wait in vain for what they would consider an appropriate gesture from an American, who emphasizes substance over style in interpersonal relations.

⊣ "What is important in Japan is not so much the deed or the result as the intent," one Japanese man said. "If the intent is good and honorable, an undesired result will be tolerated if not ignored. If I err, I should apologize sincerely, and I expect this apology to be accepted." |⊸

Failure to perceive the importance of the gesture — in this case the apology — caused confusion several years ago when the Japanese government officially expressed its regret for the incident involving Japanese terrorists at the Tel Aviv airport.

"Westerners may wonder why the government must apologize, but we have a sense of collective responsibility. We expected that our apology would be accepted; instead some people considered it an admission of legal liability and demanded compensation," a Japanese man said.

Another example of the importance of the gesture is the introduction of a prospective spouse to one's parents. Though the *deito* (date) is becoming increasingly popular in Japan, it is still considered bad form not to secure the parents' acceptance of, or at least acquiescence in, an approaching marriage.

If proper form is followed — the all-important gesture of the introduction — there is less chance of friction between the spouse and the in-laws.

One independent-minded student who did not particularly like the idea of prior parental approval admitted that he would probably still follow the proper form.

"Even I don't want to cause friction," he said.

As they have done with virtually everything they have borrowed from other cultures, the Japanese have molded the *deito* to fit their own cultural pattern. Family friends can arrange an *omiai* (meeting) which, if mutally acceptable to the boy and girl, will often be followed by a series of *deitos.* The *omiai,* though, is tentative ("One can always cancel it," a Japanese woman said.), allowing the desired delay before any final commitment.

Japanese parents seem to be satisfied with this East/West hybrid of premarital mores.

"Parents will be very happy if their very nice daughter can have a very nice boy friend," one Japanese woman said.

If such an arrangement should lead to marriage, how will the couple reconcile the relatively recent drive towards equality for women with the traditional Japanese family pattern, in which the husband is master of the house?

 "Traditionally, the Japanese woman has always followed the man, even while taking a walk. He was always first; she was last. The order in which the family bathes has been father, son, daughter, mother," a Japanese woman said.

One early crusader for greater rights for women told of her difficulties in trying to interest office co-workers in her mission.

"I told the girls that if the men asked them to bring them tea and cigarettes, they should tell the men to get them themselves. This worked for one day. Then the men complained that they were not acting like women, which is so important for a Japanese woman. Men don't like talkative, aggressive women. They may admire them, but they prefer submissive women," she said.

Since World War II, however, women have secured greater educational and job opportunities and have increasingly insisted on equal pay for equal work.

Yet it is often the *right* to a job and equal pay that is of more significance than the actual job itself, according to one Japanese woman. "Once women are secure in the knowledge that they have equal rights, they often don't use these rights. If a company agrees to give a woman a job with equal pay, she may not take it; but if there is no opportunity, she will be angry and may push on," said the woman, who estimated that probably 60 percent of Japanese women do not work outside the home.

Because the afterhours party or visit to the geisha house is considered an important factor in a man's success in the business world, the understanding wife is expected to cheerfully send her husband off for the evening.

"It would be childlike of her to appear jealous," a Japanese man said.

"A Japanese woman doesn't necessarily favor this arrangement, but she accepts it. She then rationalizes: In order for him to be successful in business, he must go to these social functions," added a Japanese woman.

Western eyes are deceived, however, if they see the Japanese wife as a helpless victim of her husband's whim, for she is confident that she is really in control.

"Women in Japan know they are the boss but pretend they are not the boss. They're very clever, I guess," said a Japanese woman coyly.

Coloring nearly all interpersonal relationships in Japan are the concepts of *on* and *giri* — "two sides of the same coin" in the words of one Japanese.

Impossible to translate satisfactorily into English, *on* signifies an indebtedness or burden which one carries for past favors done for him. *Giri* connotes the obligation to repay this indebtedness.

"*On* and *giri* are the lubricators of our society. If one has incurred an obligation, it must be repaid at one time or another in one form or another," a Japanese man said.

An orphan brought up by a generous uncle, a man loaned money by a sympathetic friend, a student influenced by an inspiring teacher — all are instances where the recipient feels an *on-giri* relationship with his benefactor.

"A teacher who was instrumental in making me what I am today retired recently, and his pupils held a fund-raising campaign to build a bust for him. I felt I had a *giri* to do that," said a successful Japanese executive.

"Even those students not particularly attached to him felt an obligation to give the same amount. I had to keep my donation at a reasonable level, so the others wouldn't feel compelled to match a substantial amount of money," he said.

The leveling effect of American egalitarianism can come as a rude jolt to the newly arrived Japanese.

"People engaged in the services were impolite; the quality of service was very low," said a Japanese man in discussing his first impressions of the U.S. "But I was soon to learn that this was characteristic of a democratic society; the people feel essentially equal.

"We see the barber in Japan as very polite and unmistakably servile. In the U.S. one finds the barber friendly, almost intimate, and possibly rude. He doesn't treat you as his master," he said.

"Service in Japan is now deteriorating; our societies are becoming similar. We used to complain that American taxi drivers wouldn't acknowledge our comments, but it's the same way now in Tokyo. One would be surprised if taxi drivers said anything," he added.

One aspect of Japanese social organization which Americans question but in some ways envy is the widespread practice of lifetime employment with the same company. The advantages are clear: recreational, medical, and retirement benefits coupled with a usually secure, comfortable existence. But the very factors which make the corporation a warm, family-like haven can lead to problems for those who lack the connections to get a good job or who fail to take some fatherly advice.

"The Japanese company is like a family, but suppose your chief suggests that you marry his daughter and you refuse. Your position with the company becomes unbearable, and it is difficult to find a comparable position elsewhere," said a Japanese student.

The security which the employment system affords the Japanese worker and the consequent restrictions on individual mobility reflect the basic ambivalence with which Japanese view their own and American society.

For to the extent that the intricate system of interpersonal relations in Japan promotes security and harmony, it necessarily impinges on personal freedom. Yet the individual liberty allowed by the informal American system leaves little room for the peaceful personal relations which the Japanese pattern fosters.

"Family life in the U.S. at first seems harsh and unfeeling compared to the close family ties in Japan. Later we come to understand the free way of thinking in the U.S.," said a Japanese woman who has lived for many years in the U.S.

"In the U.S. people don't know their neighbors, but there is a positive aspect to this as well; there is not so much concern for gossip. One can enjoy his own life without paying attention to what others are thinking of him. If we can live together peacefully with our neighbors in Japan, it is very pleasant; but if we have a quarrel, it is difficult," added another Japanese woman.

It is difficult for Westerners to understand the underlying unity among the Japanese which makes for predictable patterns of behavior.

"Because we are a compact country, it is easy to tie up the Japanese people as a single unit," was the way one Japanese woman expressed it.

"The Japanese tend to group themselves; they are not individualistic. To be in a group is a comfortable thing. Even though I am theoretically against snob groups, I must admit I am comfortable as a member of such a group," commented another Japanese woman.

"It is easy to find the pattern in Japanese life; in the U.S. everything is moving, changing," added a student.

"When I first came to the U.S., I noticed that the men seemed so tired compared to Japanese men. There was not the same sense of stability and security that is always working in Japan to promote inner peace," said the student.

Yet the more carefree — if chaotic — mode of behavior in the U.S. has its appeal to some Japanese who feel constrained by the exacting rules of Japanese etiquette.

"In Japan we must always be on guard and ask ourselves: How are other people looking at us? If I am eating dinner at my uncle's home, I am expected to eat in a formal, attentive way, for fear that without my knowing it, his wife may look at me in a disapproving way," said a young Japanese man, who well described the challenging search for a middle road which would combine the best elements of Japanese serenity and American individuality: "Insofar as we can endure the harsh individualism, American society is very comfortable. When it becomes difficult to bear, Japan then seems so comfortable."

4

KENYA

Learning by doing was an established Kenyan custom long before it was "discovered" by American educator John Dewey, and the spirit of the Ten Commandments permeated Kenyan family life well in advance of the arrival of the first Christian missionary. Divorce is virtually unknown in Kenya, and community cooperation exists to such an extent that an orphan rarely lacks a willing provider.

Yet the unwarranted stereotype of Africa as the "Dark Continent" is so firmly implanted in many parts of the world that Kenyans in the U.S. and elsewhere must endure such questions as: "Do you have houses there? Do you have streets?"

"The Hollywood image persists – that Africans are beating drums and running around in the bush amid elephants, snakes, and baboons. Some people don't believe that we have any modern facilities: roads, universities, modern communications," one Kenyan said.

Fortunately, modernization has not yet spoiled the natural beauty of a country noted for its wildlife, palm-fringed beaches, and clear lakes and rivers.

"You can draw water from the rivers and it will be safe for drinking; you can swim without any hazard," said one Kenyan proudly.

Because the Kenyan image of Americans is often formed by the long-haired, casually dressed young people that roam from one Kenyan town to another mingling freely with the people, Kenyans are surprised not to find more hippies in the U.S.

"I saw one or two demonstrating near the White House, but they looked healthy and well-to-do," one Kenyan noted.

The American tendency to give children considerable freedom in decision-making is uncommon in Kenya.

"We are strict on the discipline of our children. Loose talk when the elderly are around is considered impolite," one Kenyan said.

"This is the way we were brought up. Nothing can give a young man more of a bad reputation than to show disrespect to an older person. The old are our leaders; they are expected to know what is best," added another.

When an elderly person arrives at home, the children always take from him whatever he might be carrying; the parent himself never places it on the floor or table.

Since sons and daughters are expected to take care of their parents until their dying day, society looks with extreme disfavor on a man with means who neglects his filial obligations. A truly wayward child might receive the ultimate disgrace — the parental curse.

"I have not met any African group that does not fear the curse from a mother or father, and I never have seen one instance of a cursed person whose life went well," one Kenyan said.

A special type of companionship often develops between a boy and his grandfather or a girl and her grandmother.

"The grandfather is almost like a brother; the boy can discuss things with him that he could not discuss with his father, and the girl can do the same with her grandmother," a Kenyan commented.

"We do not think that you Americans are cruel, but merely individualistic. We still take care of the old with pleasure. It can become a burden, sometimes it pinches, but we still do it with joy," another man added.

Raised in an age when word of mouth took the place of textbooks, the older Kenyan was forced to commit everything to memory. The extent of this stored-up knowledge can startle a youthful student, who must scurry to his books to bolster a faltering memory.

"A man 60 years old can recall the smallest details of everything for the last 40 years; he has an educational system within himself. He can speak in parables and use figures of speech that we can't even make sense out of, even though we know the meanings of the individual words," said a young Kenyan man.

Because the extended family is the basis of the Kenyan way of life, successful individuals feel compelled to come to the aid of their struggling relatives.

"I am not bound by any law, but I feel it is my duty to help those unfortunate brothers who have not made it. This extends even to cousins and beyond," was the way one Kenyan explained it.

Though the husband is the recognized leader of the family, the wife's role is a central and essential one, and she occupies a "position of reverence" in the words of one Kenyan.

"Some people have criticized us for allegedly placing the woman in a lowly position, but we have not done this. Actually she is the pillar of the house and is supposed to teach children proper modes of behavior. Every activity of the family should revolve around the mother, who should cook, rear the children, and make the home a real happy place," one Kenyan said.

"Western women like to impose themselves on men, but even the educated women in Kenya frown on women who nag and boss their husbands," he added.

A Kenyan student who has lived in both a wealthy suburban area and a poor inner-city section of the U.S. sees suburban family life as somewhat akin to that in Kenya.

"There seems to be a tendency for families who are better off to be more close-knit than those struggling to survive. The family will sit down to dinner together and have time to discuss family problems. This resembles our family practice in Kenya," he said.

Beguiled by the belief that America is a country where "money flows like wine," the Kenyan is confounded by the gap between wealth and poverty which exists in the U.S.

"I think the poorest people I have ever seen are in the U.S. — both in human and material terms," the student said.

"The poorer people must struggle for their food, work night and day, and maybe try to take some classes. They don't have the chance to sit down and eat together; there's no time," he added.

"In Kenya the pace is slower. Whether rich or poor, nobody is that worried about where his next meal is coming from. My grandfather had five wives. If I visited one grandmother and she had no food, I went to another one. She would take care of any of the grandchildren. This great spirit keeps the people together," he said.

Kenyans are troubled by what they view as a curt, unfeeling approach to interpersonal relations among Americans, who are "always in a hurry going nowhere" in the words of one Kenyan.

"Unless you ask an American a question, he will not even look at you. He is occupied with his own business; individualism is very high," he added.

Encounters between Kenyans entail a much more elaborate ritual. A welcoming handshake will be followed by a series of questions about home life and mutual friends and an offer of food or drink, often tea.

"It is impolite to refuse a cup of tea. You should at least taste it to show that you appreciate the offer," one Kenyan said.

"Americans appear to us rather distant. They are not really as close to other people — even fellow Americans — as Americans overseas tend to portray. It's almost as if an American says, 'I won't let you get too close to me'; it's like building a wall," added another Kenyan.

"Unless you know someone, you can feel very lonely, very unwanted, but it is difficult to make friends unless you are introduced. At home, you can find someone to talk to in a bar. In the U.S. people come and concentrate on their beer," commented one Kenyan.

The whole question of drinking beer is not taken lightly in Kenya, and the introduction of a young man to the pleasures — and problems — of alcohol is, as one Kenyan put it, "a very solemn act."

In at least one tribe, the ceremony cannot take place until the young man is married and supposedly mature enough to drink responsibly. If the father does not personally introduce his son, he will choose a respected village elder, one who is of good temperament even while drinking, for it is believed that the young man takes after the temperament of the man who introduces him to beer.

"It's like asking him to be a foster father. He will bless the beer, ask that no harm come on the young man, and warn against drunkenness," one Kenyan explained.

When they wanted rain to come, the elders of this same tribe would go to a large bush to pray.

"The old men assembled near the center of the bush, and the old women on the periphery. We young people were not allowed into the vicinity, unless the old men wanted something brought to them. Then we would go and hand it to the women. We feared that if we played around this sacred place, we would die," recalled one Kenyan.

Perhaps no Kenyan custom causes as much confusion among outsiders as the practice of polygyny. Those who do not understand the communal approach to life among Kenyans tend to feel sorry for the women, who appear oppressed by the self-seeking males. They would be surprised to learn that it is usually the wife who suggests to her husband that he seek another mate.

Tradition has taught that a man may have as many wives as he can support and that the larger one's family, the better it is for the tribe as a whole. Males are brought up to think in terms of extending their love to several women, whom they will regard as companions and members of one big family. Girls are taught how to share a husband's love and to look upon him as the father of a single family.

"The first wife will be happy if there are several other wives. All the children are brothers and sisters. Of course, the wife may say, 'We don't have enough money to get a second wife.' Economic thinking has entered into the situation quite a bit," one Kenyan said.

"It seems to us more fair for men to marry more than one wife than to run around with other girls and have mistresses, for if you have several wives you are responsible for each and every one of them and all the children. Provisions are made for the children if one mother dies," added another man.

Some tribes do not even have a word for "unmarried" or "old maid" — so rare is the case of an unwed Kenyan.

Future husband and wife will often first meet at a dancing festival. Each girl is escorted by an older boy, usually from the same family or tribe.

"He acts like a big brother and is responsible for the girl from the time he calls for her before the dance. If anything happens to the girl, he is answerable," one Kenyan explained.

"We don't encourage a girl to have many boyfriends, though it is good for a girl to be able to handle herself socially in a group of boys," he added.

If a boy befriends more than one girl, he will usually try to conceal it from his parents.

"They don't want you to be seen with one girl today and another tomorrow. They want you to pick one and treat her well," said one Kenyan.

Once a young man has selected a prospective bride, an intricate intrigue follows.

"He will try to get friends who live near the girl to find out as much about her as they can. She doesn't know she's being observed. That's the best way to know about a person, there are no put-ons," a Kenyan student said.

If a favorable report is forthcoming, the young man will tell his parents who will transmit his interest to the girl and her family. If she wishes to pursue the matter, she will send her own "spies" into action to check out the young man's reputation and manners.

Even the young are often involved in this mutual background check.

"Once when I was a boy, I had to sit in a tree to watch my uncle's prospective bride at work in the field. I was told to count how many times she sat down when she was supposed to be working," a Kenyan recalled.

This highly controlled situation cannot, of course, exist in an impersonal urban environment, and a move to the city by the young teacher, government official, or nurse makes for a more independent life style than the traditional rural setting affords.

Schooled in the British educational style ("Just keep quiet and absorb," in the words of one Kenyan), the newly arrived student is surprised by the informal air of the American classroom.

"American students have no respect for the teacher as a teacher; he's just like anybody else. But teachers place themselves in that position, when, for example, they date the girls they are teaching," one Kenyan student said.

The mandatory nature of tipping in the U.S. irks some Kenyans, who feel that the waiter is more interested in their money than in pleasing them with his service.

"Waiters extend courtesy to get a bigger tip or because the manager is around. They are very impersonal; it's just a job to them," one Kenyan commented.

Americans can unknowingly offend if they call a Kenyan with an upturned hand, for proper Kenyan etiquette demands that the palm be face down when the calling motion is made. Shrugging the shoulders is also considered rude.

The relationship between Kenyans and black Americans presents, as one Kenyan tactfully phrased it, "a very delicate question."

"There is a closer feeling between the two than in the past. Before, black Americans depended only on what white Americans told them about Kenya. Now they have a chance to find out for themselves," said one Kenyan student, who told how black Americans on his campus had sided with Africans to protest a proposed hike in fees for foreign students.

Some Kenyans, though, disapprove of what they consider excessive pride on the part of black Americans of their African roots — when they see American blacks acting more African than the Africans.

"Black Americans and Africans have to understand one another's background better," said one Kenyan, pointing out that there is still much ignorance of Africa among most Americans — black and white.

"Personal contacts should be increased between Africans and Americans to bring about an awareness of the tremendous development that is now taking place in Africa. Much still needs to be done to educate the ordinary man about the Africa of today as compared to the old image of the time when Africa was described as the 'Dark Continent,' " he said.

5

TURKEY

Ali, a young Turkish boy, was chopping wood one morning before going to school. Suddenly the hatchet glanced off the piece of wood before him and tore into Ali's thumb, nearly splitting it off. Somehow suppressing the pain, he wrapped an old bandage around the thumb and trudged off to school as usual.

An American teaching at the school was understandably alarmed by the prospect of Ali's losing his thumb, but she was equally impressed by the intense mixture of stoicism and pride which had impelled him to conceal the hurt.

"It was killing him inside, but he was no doubt thinking, 'I have to show them that I'm a tough Turk,' " she explained.

"The Turks are a very proud people," emphasized a young Turkish woman, who has lived for many years in the United States. In her view, Turks and Americans share a tough, independent pride which must compete with certain feelings of inadequacy for supremacy in the national psyche.

"The two nations seem to suffer from superiority-inferiority complexes. Americans feel that they live in a great, generous nation but are disturbed that they do not have a culture like the British or the French. Turks take pride in the past glory of the Ottoman Empire when Turkey ruled a great part of the world, yet they were stunned when Ataturk told them that they had to Westernize, to take off the fez and put on the fedora," she said.

A natural outgrowth of this independent pride of both peoples is a stress on self-reliance, flexibility, and improvisation. Yet the dictates of industrial development have to some extent diverted the American from the traditional pattern and eased him into the role of specialist. Turks coming to the U.S. in recent years are thus surprised by the American's compartmentalized approach to knowledge.

"This specialization is beyond their immediate comprehension, and they might ask an American worker, 'Is this all you do?' Or if Turks ask a professor who specializes in potatoes a question about eggplants and he doesn't know the answer, they think: 'This is the same family of plant; why doesn't he know?' " said a Turkish man, who has worked with Americans and Turks for many years.

Like many other visitors, Turks find the American accent on punctuality and precise programming somewhat difficult to adjust to. This is particularly true for a Turk from the countryside.

"His daily life is quiet and easy, but the moment he comes to the U.S., he feels that he is entering an entirely different world. He faces a program which says 'do this, do that,' and he must force himself to be on time and stick right to the program. He should have some free time at first, to get a feel for the atmosphere on his own," advised one Turkish man.

The American's strict concept of legalism, particularly regarding traffic regulations, is also quickly noted.

"Once we were out in a rural area in the middle of nowhere and saw an American come to a stop sign. He could see for two miles in both directions, and there was no traffic coming, but he still stopped," recalled one Turk.

The casualness of certain American manners catches the Turks' attentions, as, for example, when a woman goes to the store with her hair in curlers.

"The toiletry of a woman is as private as her courtship in Turkey. Beauty shops have screens to shield their customers from outside view, and one never sees a woman with hair curlers. Women don't comb their hair or put on makeup in public, and they never smoke on the street," one Turk said.

But appropriate behavior is obviously in the eye of the beholder. For in Turkey a man might throw his coat over his pajamas and go to the store, whereas the American would consider it inappropriate to wear pajamas outside the home.

Despite the outward informality of much of American life, Turks sense a lack of warmth and emotional involvement. Paradoxically, the seemingly more affectionate Turkish behavior is played out against the backdrop of a more formal system of manners.

Thus a Turkish woman, who appreciates many aspects of American informality, arrived at the following paradox:

"Turkey seems more relaxed yet more rigid. It's hard to put your finger on it.

"A lot of things are very ceremonial in Turkey, and the *approach* is important," she added.

When Turks go to visit friends, the first five minutes will involve nothing but greetings. There will be questions about health and family, men will kiss other men on the cheeks, and women will do the same with women. A man will shake a woman's hand or bend slightly from the waist.

"It's more than a nod and not quite a bow," according to a young American woman who lived for some time in Turkey.

The visitor will be offered coffee or tea, followed by cigarettes and candy. After a second cup of tea and cookies, he will be given some lemon-scented cologne to rub on his hands.

"In Turkey we don't ask, 'Do you want coffee?' but rather 'How will you take your coffee?' " said a young Turkish woman.

Since it is considered bad manners to accept the first offer of food or drink, Turks understand that the host will make several offers and that the recipient will gradually ease into acceptance, but in the U.S. they have to learn to accept right away.

One young Turkish woman had some words of advice for her sister about to leave for the United States:

"Don't be polite in America. If you say 'No,' you'll get up from the table hungry."

The demands of Turkish formality can be irksome, however, to the American in Turkey.

"I'm used to dealing with people on a one-to-one basis and acting in an informal way, but in Turkey you must follow formal procedures — shake hands and kiss on the cheeks and bring chocolate when you go visiting. From the American viewpoint, these are games you have to play," said an American who lived several years in Turkey.

But the Turks view these "games" as important indicators of the depth of interpersonal relationships.

"Greeting is an emotional process, and you can judge the extent of closeness by the way people shake hands and hug one another. In the U.S. people shake hands, but you don't know how they really feel about one another," said a Turkish man.

The Turkish language reflects this emotional, affectionate approach, and an American who lived in Turkey found certain sentences warmer and more expressive in Turkish than in English.

"We might say, 'Drive safely and have a good trip.' The Turks would say something that would connote, 'A good trip, God's blessings, a safe journey, and Godspeed' all tied together. Or after a good supper, instead of merely saying 'thank you,' Turks would say, 'God's blessings on your hands,' since the hands prepared the delicious meal," she said.

There are different types of greetings, depending on the relationship of those involved. A young woman would kiss the hand of an older woman and put it to her forehead. The older woman would call the younger *canim* ("dear" or "my beloved"), but not in a condescending way. In addressing someone in a formal way, the word *efendi* ("sir" or "lady") is attached to the person's name. If the one being spoken to has a prestigious job, the word *bey* ("sir") is added to the name.

Because hugging and kissing play such an important part in Turkish greeting, American conduct appears unduly restrained to the Turks.

"It looks funny to us to see a father and son only shaking hands," one Turk said.

A Turkish girl who had spent several months in the U.S. shocked her friends when she merely waved to them instead of hugging them, thereby showing her rapid "Americanization," and a Turkish woman recalled how her friend was amused to see sensitivity training (a form of group therapy in which participants are urged to act out their emotions) in the U.S.

"Look at the Americans. They pay money to learn to touch one another," she said.

American friendship appears casual and lacking in depth to the Turks, who demand more in reciprocal obligations.

"When you make friends in Turkey, you put yourself under an obligation. You commit yourself to your friend and expect a commitment from him; it's very rigid," said one Turk.

"You're a slave to your friend, but your friend is a slave to you," was the way another Turk expressed it.

Because the relationship is so all-encompassing and the emphasis is on sharing, Turks are troubled by the individualistic aspects of American behavior, particularly the American concept of privacy.

"Time for yourself — privacy — is important in the United States, but this concept doesn't exist in Turkey. The worst thing in the U.S. is loneliness. In Turkey you can just show up at a friend's house, but I get intimidated in the U.S. because the American might say, 'I want to read a book or watch TV.' The straightforwardness of Americans — the way they will say, 'I can't do that today' — really gets to you," said a young Turkish woman.

"Americans ask themselves, 'How much of my time is it going to take?' Sometimes I can't stand the word 'time,' " she added.

Americans who live in Turkey, however, find the lack of privacy difficult to adjust to.

"People would walk right in my door without knocking," one American said.

"Americans feel crowded by Turkish behavior. Turks will think that the poor American is lonely, and all the neighbors will drop by. This drives the American crazy," added a Turkish woman.

The open manner of exchanging gifts among Americans seems ostentatious to Turks, who give their presents in as inconspicuous a way as possible.

A Turk who goes visiting will usually bring along some candy or flowers for the hostess but will never give it to her directly.

"When the hostess is hanging up the coats, the visitor will lay the gift quietly and in a hidden manner on the table and never say a word. The hostess will not acknowledge the gift then but may say 'thank you' later," said an American who had lived in Turkey.

Thus the old Turkish proverb is fulfilled: "If your left hand gives, your right hand shouldn't know about it."

Two stereotypes that Hollywood has helped create are that all Americans are rich and that American women are loose morally.

"In Turkey we have a different concept of wealth; a man who owns a car is wealthy. In the U.S., however, one needs a car; it's as insignificant as a ballpoint pen. But Turks think, 'Everybody has a car; therefore everybody is wealthy.' This creates a barrier to understanding problems of low income people," said a Turkish man who has lived for some time in the U.S.

Particularly puzzling to the Turkish male is the freedom enjoyed by the American woman — freedom to go to movies, sit in the park, and eat in restaurants unescorted. For custom has precluded such behavior by most Turkish women.

Since the outward appearance seems frivolous and inviting to the

Turks, they find it hard to believe that such conduct can mask a rather strict morality.

"Traditionally, U.S. society has felt the influence of strong, conservative religious beliefs, but these concepts are not reflected in the American's outward appearance," was the way one Turk analyzed it. Since "dating" in Turkey is pretty much restricted to certain segments of the urban population, an American girl living outside a Turkish city has to be extremely circumspect in her conduct with the opposite sex.

"If an American boy came to visit me and I could justify that he was visiting someone else or that he was my brother, there would be minimal acceptance," said an American who lived for some time in Turkey.

"If I held hands with him, people would assume that we were getting married, and I couldn't hold hands with anyone else in the future. If I went out with a Turkish boy, people would disapprove; and if I held hands with him, I might just as well leave the country. My reputation would be absolutely shot unless an announcement was made through my employer that I was getting married," she added.

Because the family, particularly in rural Turkey, is still strongly patriarchal, Turks are surprised by the freedom of expression allowed American children.

"In Turkey whatever the father says is right, and children should obey. It's hard for Turkish children to discuss their opinions until they reach their mid-teens. In the U.S., kids have their own kingdom within the family itself," said one Turkish father.

The Turkish child receives perhaps stronger doses of both discipline and affection than his American counterpart.

"If a Turkish child falls, the parent will rush to pick him up. The American parent, on seeing his child fall, will keep an eye on him to see that he is all right, but he won't dash to pick him up. This helps him develop self-confidence," said one Turk.

Because the male is the dominant figure in the Turkish family, he is not expected to perform the chivalrous gestures that an American man would render for the woman he is escorting — such as opening the car door.

Whereas the American regards such actions as polite, the Turk tends to look on them as subservient. Thus Turks do not like to hold doors for anyone — male or female.

"There is a concept of 'position' as opposed to 'courtesy.' A man opening a door places himself in a position of inferiority. It looks like he is giving in, and the others feel they can be more demanding of him," explained a Turkish man.

Despite the patriarchal trappings of Turkish society, however, many Turks believe that an educated Turkish woman has greater access to such professions as doctor, lawyer, scientist, and professor than her American counterpart.

Traditionally, the Turkish teacher has assumed quite naturally the role of father figure. The attitude of Turkish parents as they turn their child over to the teacher is well expressed by this pithy saying: "His flesh is yours; his bones are mine."

"You're supposed to fear the teacher like you fear Allah. When he comes into the class, all stand up. When you meet him in the street, you bow. This attitude is changing to some extent as more and more people seek education, but the teacher is still treated with considerable respect," said one Turkish woman.

"A student must be serious and act like a gentleman. In the U.S. students can sit like this...," said a Turkish man, as he thrust his feet on the desk. "This may be more relaxing, and perhaps the student can grasp the idea of the teacher better, but it is not the Turkish custom."

"The teacher is still placed on a pedestal in the rural areas, but in the cities students are not afraid to speak out. The teacher's role is being redefined," added an American who had taught in Turkey.

The patriarchal pattern can also be seen in the treatment of people employed in the service occupations — waiter, driver, doorman, etc. But there seems to be some difference of opinion as to the exact relationship between the one being waited on and the one performing the service.

"If you provide services to someone in Turkey, you are considered in the servant group. The idea is that if a man is serving me, he is lower than I am. Turks can be harsh (by American standards) on waiters and waitresses unless they get to know them," said one Turk.

An American who lived in Turkey, however, found that the average Turk treated the service people well but that a wealthy man of power would be more demanding to show his importance. She also felt that a person employed in the services took a measure of pride in his work.

"If a Turk doesn't get good service, his reprimand would be like that of a father to a son, but if he tries that approach in the U.S., he will come off as aggressive," she added.

Another American who spent some time in Turkey felt that it would be "romanticizing" the situation to say that service people took pride in their jobs.

"The person performing the service is often from the countryside; he is happy to be employed. He expects to be bossed around," added a Turkish woman.

Perhaps the conduct could best be termed "patronizing" − with all the complex nuances of hierarchical haughtiness and kindly concern that the term connotes.

Once Ataturk was giving a reception for the diplomatic corps. The waiters were enlisted men in the army, mainly village boys, whose training had not included the fine points of serving table. One of them spilled a plate of fruit in the British ambassador's lap.

Ataturk, the "Father of the Turks," was undismayed.

"I taught my nation almost everything," he said, "but I could never teach them to wait on other people."

"The Turks have so much pride; but it sometimes gets in their way, and it hurts them," said an American who lived in Turkey. "Yet you can't help but admire this pride. It's such a beautiful thing, and it has carried them through tough situations."

And a Turkish man concluded: "Turks are proud and hardheaded − like Americans."

6

COLOMBIA

Though they are hemispheric neighbors and cultural cousins, Colombia and the United States have chosen decidedly different drummers to set the tempo for their respective life styles.

Accustomed to the cordiality and conviviality which a more leisurely pace affords at home, the Colombian is suddenly forced to march to an unfamiliar staccato beat when he arrives in the U.S.A.

"Emotionally we find America different — a little cold. Americans don't seem to care about other people. In Colombia we are more dependent on one another," a Colombian woman said.

"If a friend asks me to stay with her children in Colombia because the maid is gone, I will be right there even if I have other things to do. Your own life comes first in the U.S.; in Colombia it is completely reversed," she added.

Since the elaborate Colombian greeting involves shaking hands and asking questions about family and friends, the Colombian is dismayed when the American says a hurried "Hi" and is on his way.

"At the beginning this was terrible for me. I didn't know what to do with my hand, for I would extend it to shake hands and find myself grasping the air. We thought, 'These people are so cold.' It is difficult if you stay in the U.S. only a short time," commented another Colombian woman.

"Your life is so planned; everything is step by step. We are not so regimented. You are very punctual. Your watch always works. In Colombia people don't look at their watches so often," said the first woman, who recalled how her brother had asked to be *awakened* at 8 o'clock for an 8 a.m. appointment.

This difference in approach can in part be accounted for by the way in which work is viewed in the two societies.

"The tendency in the U.S. to think that life is only work hits you in the face. Work seems to be the one type of motivation," a Colombian said.

"The American is aggressive in his job; work becomes something essential to his life. The Colombian approach is more leisurely," added an American who had spent considerable time in Colombia. "The American seems to be two quite different persons. He goes to church on Sunday and takes his family for a ride in the country. Then on Monday he will do anything – crush any enemy, go to any extreme," said one Colombian, adding that his experience in the U.S. had not led him to dispel this image.

Another Colombian, who had been in the U.S. 22 years ago, noted some changes over the years.

"I was very much impressed at that time by the efficiency of the American worker. Now I have the impression that this attitude towards work is changing for the worse. People seem tired of work," he said.

The traditional stereotype that Colombians have held of the American blends elements of the indomitable superman, the cruel exploiter, and the naive innocent. One Colombian explained why he felt the general picture formed in Colombia did not necessarily conform to the reality he found in the U.S.

"We have historically felt that the American is naive, whereas we consider ourselves to have *malicia indígena* (indigenous malice) and a more complicated mind. We thought that English jokes were not as sophisticated and complicated as those in Spanish. But this image was formed from observing Americans in Colombia, without realizing that people are not themselves and are usually very cautious in a foreign country," he said.

The opposite view – that the American as imperialist is the root of all evil – oversimplifies the economic reality of competitive pricing in the U.S., in this man's opinion.

"Anything trivial for you can have meaning for us. If you see that a pound of bananas is five cents cheaper in one supermarket, you will buy those. Yet to produce bananas five cents cheaper, the manager of the banana consortium might have to do things harmful to our country – such as firing a labor union leader or reducing workers' pay," he explained.

Such incidents lead to charges of "imperialism," whereas in terms of the U.S. market structure this buying behavior is a perfectly legitimate example of comparative shopping.

There is a tendency in Colombia to believe that all Americans think the same, that the U.S. is a conformist society.

"Actually there are different points of view. The U.S. is less dogmatic and more open than we had thought," said one Colombian.

Many misunderstandings arise because of the difference in attitude of Colombians and Americans concerning the concept of service.

"Service people are more solicitous in Latin America. They do more; they show more feeling. You get the idea they don't want to serve you in the U.S. They just bring you a menu and a glass of ice water," said one Colombian.

"In Colombia there is more emphasis on being polite, attentive, and courteous. In the U.S. we are taught these things; but life is more agitated and brisk, and so the emphasis is not the same," added an American.

One Colombian who initially felt service in the U.S. to be as frigid as the glass of ice water placed unceremoniously in front of him gave a perceptive account of his increasing awareness of the differences in the two societies.

"With more experience I have observed that Americans are shy before service people; they don't feel comfortable being served. They accept almost anything and consider it bad manners to complain. Latins in general want to have good service and will complain more readily. To them, the service in the U.S. always lacks *adornos* (embellishment). They will say something not expected by the American waiter and thus seem to him out of order," he said.

"Americans don't want the other person to feel inferior because he is serving them; they want to place him on an equal plane. They feel it is just an accident that you are waiting on me and I am being waited on, for in the U.S. almost everybody will be in a service position sometime in his life — a waiter, waitress, gas station attendant, or taxi driver," he continued.

"In Latin America people will work as waiters and waitresses all their lives, and they are looked at as people in inferior positions," he added.

The more assertive attitude of the American service person can be unsettling to the newly arrived Colombian.

"A person in a high position in Colombia counts on having the service people under him to confirm his position. In the U.S. he feels uncomfortable because that is eliminated; there's a loss of well-being," said another Colombian, who commented on the transformation of a Colombian service person in the United States.

"A mechanic or *campesino* (peasant) in Colombia won't look you in the eye or shake your hand; he will only hold out his hand. After three months in the U.S. he will look you in the eye and give you a firm handshake. He has more self-respect; he has become more of a person," he said.

Working out the appropriate relationship with the maid can pose some formidable problems for the American family in Colombia.

"Colombians will ring a bell for the maid to come; Americans find this repugnant. They will get up and ask the maid to come or yell for her; this is obnoxious to Colombians," said an American who lived in Colombia for several years.

"The American will be concerned that the maid 'better herself,' develop a skill. So the maid ends up going to school three-fourths of the day and working only one-fourth. The Colombian will say: 'Why? A maid's a maid.' Americans tend to negotiate the salary with the maid rather than merely telling her what she will receive. Maids who work for Americans are ruined to work for Colombians," said the American.

"But it won't do any good to tell an American that treating the maid like this will make her future in Colombia more difficult, for he can't help acting this way," he added.

Problems of a different sort are encountered by Colombians when they bring a maid to the U.S. For in Colombia, even homes of poor families will have rooms for the maids, but Colombians look in vain for such rooms in American houses and apartments.

"It's very inconvenient. American houses don't have the correct room, so some families have to build a special room. Often the maid doesn't learn to speak English, so it is difficult for her to get along out in society," explained one Colombian.

"You become the servant of the maid. You have to take her to Spanish movies, find Spanish-speaking friends for her. Families end up waiting on the maids," he said.

Linguistic differences between Spanish and English reflect the more cordial, loquacious Colombian style and the pragmatic, direct American approach.

"When you are used to the rhythm of Spanish and don't know

English well, English sounds brusque and curt; the intonation seems strange," a Colombian said.

"We are a lot more flowery than you are," added another Colombian. "You have the concept that time is money, that time is scarce. Time is not a free good for you. The American will say 'Hello' and get right down to business. This appears impolite to us, for we like to do business in a cordial atmosphere. Actually, in terms of American society, the American is being considerate, for he does not want to waste the time of the other person."

"You're more outspoken. You say things bluntly without caring whether or not you hurt the other person's feelings, and you expect the other person to be as blunt. The Colombian will not speak so directly and will retract his words if he sees that the other person's feelings are hurt," he said.

A Colombian dentist living in the U.S. has devised an interesting division of her use of the two languages.

"I prefer to use Spanish colloquially — it's more expressive — but technically, I prefer English," she said.

The differences in the two languages are highlighted when it comes time to write a letter, for the same content that can be put in one page in English will often take two pages in Spanish. Depending on one's cultural perspective, the letter will appear curt or verbose.

"We have to explain that people writing letters in English are not impolite but that that is simply the way to say it," said a Colombian familiar with both business worlds. "In Colombia business letters are now becoming shorter," he added.

Language differences have their humorous aspects as well. Since the "b" and "v" sounds are often indistinguishable in Spanish, a failure to make the distinction required in English led to the following comment from a Colombian student of English: "My consonants are all right, but I'm having trouble with my bowels."

English dialogues studiously memorized in Colombia can prove inadequate when it comes time to put them to use in the U.S.

"We were taught to say 'Coca-Cola,' only to find that in the U.S. everyone says 'Coke.' We learned to order a 'hamburger' but weren't prepared for 'What do you want on it?' spoken so rapidly that we could not understand it. Even if we had understood, we still would not have known what to answer, for it was only later that we noticed the onions, tomatoes, catsup, etc.," said one Colombian.

A seemingly simple thing like the distance between speakers can interfere with effective communication.

"The American will stand at least a yard away from you, creating a cold atmosphere. The Colombian will stand right beside you and give you a pat on the back; it's a more cordial approach," said one Colombian.

To the American, however, the "cordial" Colombian manner will appear overpowering, and it is not uncommon to find a Colombian backing an American across the room — each speaker trying to establish the proper conversational distance.

A "generation gap" can develop between Colombian parents and their children when the family moves to the U.S., for as the teenagers seek the freedom enjoyed by their American counterparts, the parents will be striving to keep their customs.

"Discipline within the family is much stronger in Colombia than in the U.S. for both boys and girls. The first thing you notice here is trying to adjust to new standards of more freedom, especially for girls," said a Colombian father who had lived several years in the U.S.

The traditional system of chaperonage and *visitas de novio* (boy visiting the girl in her house) have recently been replaced by dating in some Colombian circles.

"We have the concept of dating, especially within the high income groups, but this is rather new and has not yet extended to most of the population," explained one Colombian man.

A Colombian woman, however, thought it was unrealistic for parents to think they could "protect" their children from American mores by sending them back to Bogotá.

"Youth at home are onto marijuana, and kids are asking, 'Why should I cut my hair?' Ten years ago you could not go out alone at night with a man, and we were never left alone with our boy friends. Now it's very much like the U.S. You can go for rides and to movies and dances alone," she said.

"*Home* life is less important, but *family* life is more important in Colombia," said one Colombian in explaining that the American spends more time at home but that family ties appear stronger in Colombia.

"The American works in the garden and repairs things around the house; he's more organized. In Colombia you arrive home late and don't do these jobs. The first time I mowed the lawn was in the U.S.," he said.

"Yet we ask ourselves, 'Since so much of life is spent together at home in the U.S., why do ties between parents and children become so weak as the children grow older?' The concept of family is broader in Colombia," he added.

"Americans seem to feel more loyalty to other organizations — the work group, sports club, university, friends — than to the family," noted another Colombian, who pointed out that the traditional extended family was also disappearing in urban areas in his country.

A streak of puritanism in the American mentality tends to prevent the carefree conviviality that marks a Colombian social event, according to an American who has spent several years in Latin America.

"In the U.S. bars are dark; they're places to hide, to escape, rooted in the idea that drinking is evil. In Latin America the atmosphere is more light and open," he said.

Yet the more straitlaced American style is not without its attractive elements.

"I admire the discipline of the American people. They respect rules of all kinds. If the street sign says, 'Don't walk,' you don't walk. Everyone respects the other person's turn in a store," said one Colombian woman.

Though the mystique of *machismo* (the masculine ideal embodying honor, romance, strength, and pride) and the male's dominant position in society have by no means completely disappeared, there have been considerable modifications — particularly among the urban elite.

"The woman's role is changing rapidly. Husbands are more liberal in letting their wives work and participate in politics," said one man.

"There is a great deal of respect for the woman, but the idea still persists that woman has certain functions and man has others. We shouldn't compete but rather be complementary; we're trying to minimize competitiveness. We haven't yet accepted the fact that a woman can manage men in the sense of an executive position," said one young Colombian man, who added that worldwide changes in the role of women had virtually eliminated *machismo* among people his age.

"The freedom of the man is greater in the rural areas. In general, it's negatively correlated with the level of income," added another Colombian.

At the same time, the *matrona* — the woman who manages her household with efficiency and discipline — is a highly respected figure in Colombian culture.

The Catholic Church, while still a prominent force in Colombian life, is no longer the final arbiter in secular matters.

"We no longer look to the Church for leadership except in religious matters, whereas we formerly considered the Church as almost a supreme court which would determine whether government action was morally right or wrong. Now the civil institutions will speak out," said one Colombian.

The concept of dealing *personally* with the highest ranking official is deeply imbedded in Colombian thought.

"We try to deal with the most important person, even for the smallest problem. If I want a scholarship for one of my sons, I must speak with the minister himself. I would be very disappointed if I had to speak first to the man actually in charge of what I want," explained one Colombian.

Obviously the minister cannot attend to every minor matter personally, but he will see every caller for at least a minute and then send him to the one actually responsible for that particular request.

"If there is a strike in a factory, both labor and management will want to come to the President directly," the man said.

"As a government official in Colombia, I could work only in the morning. In the afternoon I had to see people; I had nobody screening. I received anybody who requested an audience. This is true of all the ministers and the President," he said.

One observant Colombian discussed the philosophical outlook toward thought and action in the two societies — how an obsession with perfection serves to impede action in Colombia while a tendency to spring immediately into action hinders a planned march to a thought-out ideal in the U.S.

"We have traditionally valued conversation and have had the *mañana* idea: We'll talk about it today and act on it tomorrow. In the U.S., you just do it. We'll sit down and wait for the perfect idea," he said.

"Colombian writing is always looking towards where Colombia is going, but if you were to ask an American, 'Where are you going?', he would probably say, 'Don't ask me; I'm just going.' In Colombia, we are always reaching out for something; we don't know quite what it is."

7

INDONESIA

Roads reflect a way of life. This is the theory of an observant Indonesian, who, in comparing the highway systems in his own country and the U.S.A., highlighted patterns of behavior in the two societies.

"In the U.S. there are carefully marked lanes and strict traffic regulations which make for a fast, efficient journey. But there are restrictions and pressures too, for you can't stop wherever you want, make U-turns, or exceed the speed limit. In Indonesia you can drift from left to right, stop and turn when you feel like it. There is neither the speed nor the pressure of the American system," he said.

"Everything in the U.S. is so organized," added another Indonesian. "When newcomers see all the cars parked on the side of the road, they think there must be a party. It is hard to imagine that there could be so many cars."

"We both like and dislike the systematic organization of American society. We are trying to rush headlong into development but are apprehensive of the side effects: the lack of time for casual interaction between people, the loss of the midday siesta and leisurely pace of life," added the first man.

When an Indonesian first arrives in the U.S., many of the stereotypes he has brought with him concerning American society are readily confirmed. The luxurious houses, modern roads and schools, fancy cars and television sets have been noted in numerous Hollywood movies. But there are surprises as well, particularly for visitors whose first stop is Washington, D.C.

"I thought things would be better, cleaner, more impressive. I was surprised to see that not all the roads were good and was disappointed in the residential quarters until I went to the suburbs," said one Indonesian, whose wife had felt less than welcome on her first visit to an American department store.

"When she went to pay with a check, she had to stand in front of a camera. She felt like a common criminal and cancelled all her purchases. We later found out that such an identification procedure was necessary and that it was not just for foreigners," he said.

"Living is not a matter of survival in the U.S. Most people work not just for today but for the future. But as one stays longer, he is exposed to the gaps — the poorer pockets of the country, the lack of a viable health care system for all economic levels," one man said.

An Indonesian woman was distressed by the amount of food Americans throw away.

"Every one of my friends has noticed this; we are conditioned to eat everything on our plates. We are also surprised to see bottles, containers, and newspapers put in the garbage, for we would sell them to the junk man," she said.

The approach to interpersonal relations can easily lead to mutual misunderstanding. It is as difficult for the Indonesian to comprehend the direct, open American style as it is for the American to fathom the subtleties of the Indonesian — particularly the Javanese — psyche.

"Americans are very friendly, open, and polite, but we don't know whether they mean it. We cannot tell," said one Indonesian who had studied at an American university.

"The atmosphere at a sorority party would look very intimate, but if the same people met on the street, they might just ignore one another. Americans look warm, but when a relationship starts to become personal, they try to avoid it.

"We don't differentiate between colleagues and friends. Once we know someone in any capacity, he is a friend. In the U.S. a distinction is made between an official, business relationship and a personal relationship," he said.

"Some Indonesians like this direct, open approach; others find it difficult to get used to. Indonesians are not direct by nature," said another man.

"The Javanese especially tend to be subtle. They might be suspicious of what the American is up to, for the American is so open that it seems he must have an ulterior motive. The Javanese doesn't want to commit himself until he is absolutely sure," added an Indonesian woman.

If the Indonesians have trouble probing beneath the Americans' effervescence, Americans experience a similar stumbling block when confronted with Indonesian indirection.

A sensitive Indonesian student described how an American might view a typical Indonesian: "He would appear extremely cautious in his behavior and movements and not seem at ease or relaxed. There would be a lot of artificiality in his physical behavior, and he would appear indirect and evasive."

"It seems to Americans that Indonesians can't make up their minds. Americans are always saying, 'It's so hard to pin them down,' " added an Indonesian woman.

The casual American friendship pattern contrasts sharply with the intense, permanent relationship which characterizes Indonesian culture.

"The degree of demand and the give and take is almost limitless," noted an Indonesian student.

"When you are friendly to Indonesians, they will make demands on you. But they will return the favor if you ask them," said an American who had lived in Indonesia.

Recently arrived Indonesians are somewhat surprised by the Americans' casual manner of dress, for in Indonesia one's status can generally be determined from the cut of his clothes.

"One might think that because an American is dressed simply, he is from the lower class. But you can't tell from his dress; he might be anybody," one Indonesian said.

In another sense, the Indonesian appears casual to the clock-controlled American.

"In the U.S. a 4 o'clock appointment really means 4 o'clock, but to an Indonesian half an hour doesn't mean much. We always have to specify whether we mean 'Indonesian' or 'American' time," an Indonesian woman said.

"The official hours of work in Indonesia are from 7 to 1 o'clock, but an official might come at 9 o'clock and go home at noon so as not to miss the bus," added another woman.

The Javanese, particularly, would rather live for today than worry about tomorrow, and they believe that a leisurely pace has its own rewards. "We do it slowly, but we achieve it, rather than doing it quickly and not getting there" is a rough English approximation of a well-known Javanese saying.

Because the Indonesian language lends itself more to qualitative descriptions and discussions of concepts than to specific, quantitative details, the American's ready use of statistical measurement is a source of surprise — and often amusement — to the general-minded Indonesian. "Not many people in Djakarta would know what the temperature is right now. Americans would not only know the temperature but might even be able to attribute it to a low pressure front. Even during American football games, the announcer keeps telling how many times a player has carried the ball, how many yards he has gained, the number of complete and incomplete passes, etc.," said one Indonesian, who pointed out that until he was in high school he knew only that his father "worked in an office."

The American's free use of complimentary phrases and terms of endearment seems effusive to the Indonesian, raised in an atmosphere where self-conscious restraint is the rule.

"We are not used to praising people. If someone says, 'You look beautiful,' it is considered crude. The recipient would be annoyed," an Indonesian man said.

When an American — particularly a male — refers to an Indonesian woman as "dear" or "honey," the initial reaction is that he is being overly forward.

"At first, when an American would say, 'You have a nice dress,' I was at a loss for words. I gradually learned how to respond — simply say 'thank you' — by listening to Americans," one woman said.

Coming from a society where silence needs no explanation and politeness is gauged by the softness of speech, Indonesians would like to turn down the volume of most American voices. Americans, for their part, despair of ever raising Indonesian utterances above a whisper.

"When I lived with a family in Topeka, Kansas, my American 'mother' kept saying, 'Speak up, we can't hear you.' She thought I was being impolite," said one woman who had participated in the American Field Service high school exchange program.

Shaped by the Socratic tradition of give-and-take questioning, the American prizes precise, analytical discussion. But such an approach often seems overly direct and needlessly verbose to the more intuitive Indonesian.

"In the U.S. everything has to be talked about and analyzed. Even the littlest thing has to be 'why? why? why?' I get a headache from such persistent questions," said an Indonesian woman, who described how an American and an Indonesian mother might react if they were alone with their sons as the sun was going down. "If the child said, 'What a beautiful sunset,' the American mother would probably say, 'Why is it a beautiful sunset?' The Indonesian mother wouldn't say anything."

The same woman saw at least one advantage, though, to the American style. "Kids are brought up to question; we're not raised to ask reasons for things."

"Indonesian children are taught to revere God, their parents, and their teacher in that order. These are their mentors, and they would never have the gall to refute the rightness of the teacher," one Indonesian said.

"In Indonesia the teacher is to be followed not only academically but also morally. This demands too much of a teacher. If he makes a mistake, he is judged twice as hard as a nonteacher," commented another Indonesian.

Though they are unaccustomed to speaking out in class, many Indonesian students find the U.S. seminar style "refreshing and stimulating" according to one Indonesian woman.

Yet it still seems strange to many Indonesians that a teacher would grade on the basis of class discussion, and a student pointed out that the popular late evening "talk shows" on U.S. television — "where the people do nothing but talk for two hours" — would be unheard of at home.

"The chief complaint of American teachers in Indonesia is that the students do not respond, that they expect the teachers to think for them," added an Indonesian woman.

Perhaps nowhere do Indonesian and American attitudes stand out in sharper contrast than in the area of decision-making and conflict resolution. Indeed the democratic American process, which highlights competing views and majority rule, is completely alien to the Indonesian concept of *musjawarah* — an intricate series of consensus-reaching agreements culminating in a unanimous decision.

"Open disagreement is avoided like the plague, and we frown on the factions that exist in the U.S. What Americans regard as a frank, open political discussion, we view as shocking, recriminating, and impolite. I still can't stand a hard-hitting argument," said an Indonesian woman living in the U.S.

"If the American political system were brought to Indonesia, the whole country would be torn apart. To us, a 50-percent-plus-one decision doesn't necessarily mean that the truth has been attained; the result could be false. We believe that if you can't agree to all points, you should at least agree to some points; this is in our blood," added another Indonesian.

Contributing to this communal approach is the concept of *gotong royong*, which connotes a working together or mutual aid.

"We share everything together — even our poverty. For when we share, everybody is poor. If someone just came and knocked on my door, I would let him in. An American woman was surprised when her Indonesian husband invited in a distant relative from a faraway city. He hadn't sent a letter before; he just dropped in," explained an Indonesian man.

The small, self-contained nuclear family unit — now the dominant domestic pattern in the U.S. — suggests loose ties between relatives to the average Indonesian.

"We tend to think that if you don't know your second cousin, you're not civilized, you have no warmth in you," said one young Indonesian whose parents now house approximately 20 people.

"One of the negative effects of development is that people don't have time for their families. Yet we are extreme to the degree of suffocation; I feel myself confined and engulfed by family on all sides. This is not conducive to productivity; we just sit around. On the other hand, it is a warm relationship, and no one ever gets sent to an old-age home," he said.

The child-centered manner of raising a family in the U.S. seems to deprive parents of their rightful authority, for to Indonesians a child should be seen and not heard.

"It comes as a shock to us to see a child talking back to his mother or father. In Indonesia this is a sin of the first order," according to an Indonesian woman.

"Americans give their children considerable freedom, but in Indonesia one is considered a child until he is married. Until then, he is the responsibility of the parents," added an Indonesian man.

Unlike the egalitarian Indonesian tongue, the traditional Javanese language features an intricate hierarchical system of five levels (six counting a combination version to be used between levels), which must be mastered through socialization and/or study of literary classics.

"When two Javanese meet for the first time, they try to determine each other's status by inquiring about parents, occupation, and schooling. When each knows the other's slot, they will proceed," explained a Javanese woman.

The Dutch, who controlled the coastal areas during the colonial period, pushed the Javanese kingdoms inward, then pretty much left them alone. Thus there was plenty of time to hone the language levels to perfection.

Such is no longer the case, and the younger generation — schooled in the Indonesian tongue — is finding it increasingly difficult to speak Javanese well.

Underlying the hierarchical and egalitarian aspects of the languages, moreover, is a profound soul-searching as to whether a traditional stratified society can be comfortably changed to a more egalitarian order. And if such a transition is indeed possible, many Indonesians wonder whether it is really desirable.

Some Indonesians — and this would probably be particularly true of the older generation — seem satisfied with the traditional hierarchy.

"Americans have the egalitarian concept deep in their hearts, but our country has degrees," was the way one man expressed it.

"We are different in our way of living and way of thinking. We have our own pattern of thought and idea of what society should be," added another man.

Yet the younger generation appears anxious to change the existing order. One young man, for example, referred to stratification as a "historical burden."

"The only hierarchy I could accept is a hierarchy by merit. Islam does not recognize a hierarchy. Thus democracy is present in Indonesia in certain traditions but submerged by other traditions. Consequently there is a value conflict within Indonesia itself," he said.

A young woman painted a vivid picture of the existing structure, then expressed some personal reservations.

"Indonesians are not programmed to think that people are equal. A servant is a servant no matter how clever or bright he may be. You can treat him well, be kind to him, but he should know his place. Yet the servants themselves don't mind. They accept this position and don't have any ambition to advance to a higher position," she said.

"Indonesians from the higher classes would never consider dating or marrying someone from the lower class. The respect the lower class has for its masters is very overt, very obvious. I'm getting disappointed and sick of it myself," she concluded.

"We have to go very slowly (toward egalitarianism). We have to be elitist or hierarchical to some degree. But it should be strongly remembered that this is just a transition, while we are waiting for the education to catch up," said a young man.

Yet somewhere between the supporters of stratification and the proponents of egalitarianism exists an admittedly ambivalent position, typified by the following comments from a member of "the lowest level of the aristocracy."

"I was in the forefront of the revolution. I was against the Dutch and the aristocrats associated with the Dutch. But I now see certain values in the feudal times which we think we might be losing — respect for authority, the concept of sportsmanship as epitomized by the strong, wise *satria* (knight) ready to help the poor," this man said.

The egalitarian aspects of the struggle against the Dutch had important implications concerning the role of women.

"In the revolutionary period men and women were on almost equal ground. Some women were commanders of resistance against the Dutch — commanders on the battlefield," emphasized an Indonesian.

"The freedom of women in Indonesia is a function of economic dependence. On the highest level, it is a function of education and social status," said one Indonesian, who felt that it was easier for Indonesian males to work under a woman's supervision than it was for American men.

A distinction must be drawn between the independence of the educated, urban woman and the more subordinate position of her rural counterpart. Employment barriers are virtually nonexistent for the former — given the heavy demand for highly qualified personnel of either sex.

The rural woman, on the other hand, actually appears to lose a measure of her economic independence as she moves up socially. For the inherent equality which exists when a woman works alongside her husband in the field quickly disappears when the man moves on to a more prestigious job.

"If a man becomes a government official, the community will no longer consider it proper for his wife to work as a farmer. She will be expected to be more of a lady, thus losing her independent economic role and her position of equality within the family. She becomes a housewife, which connotes 'Stay in the back and no decision-making,' " commented an Indonesian woman.

Beneath this facade of subordination, however, the Indonesian woman may exert considerable influence.

"She controls in a subtle way" was the way one Indonesian woman summed it up.

"Our women are stronger than outsiders may think, but it is simply not our tradition to shout things out, and thus they may appear subordinate," added a young man.

Though divorce is looked on with extreme disfavor by the educated elite, it is widely practiced in the countryside. Women's organizations, concerned about the plight of the rural wife, are trying to effect passage of a marriage law which will give her greater rights.

Mention should be made, however, of the Minangkabau society of West Sumatra, whose matriarchal structure provides for inheritance through the female line. Minangkabau males supposedly waste no time in seeking mates from other regions, notably Java.

Unlike many of the outer-islanders, the Javanese tend to emphasize moderation and synthesis both in their beliefs and in their emotional reactions.

"The Javanese don't express themselves in very sharp terms. We are trained to control ourselves as much as possible, but at the same time we are expected to read expressions in others' faces. Non-Javanese thus seem more dynamic," noted one Javanese, who commented that the lines between Christian, Moslem, and Buddhist beliefs tend to be blurred and that the Javanese take something from all of them.

Coupled with this sense of restraint is a desire not to displease or offend, a heightened sensitivity to proper and improper conduct. Though Indonesian Embassy personnel could disobey "No Parking" signs with impunity, they are careful to adhere to them.

"In a country where we are the guests, we should behave like guests and not take advantage of special privileges," one Indonesian said.

Whereas the American has a sense of individual responsibility and accompanying feelings of guilt, the Indonesian thinks first of the society as a whole and experiences shame if his conduct deviates from the group norm.

This underlying difference in cultural patterns between East and West in general, and Indonesia and the U.S. in particular, was simply yet profoundly illustrated by a perceptive Indonesian: "In the West, the individual is the totality; whereas in the East, the totality is the cosmos. Americans are 210 million individuals, but we are one."

8

ETHIOPIA

A leader of the Ethiopian Church came to the United States to seek assistance in technical and industrial arts training from American church groups. Academicians and theologians assembled to hear his request, apparently eager to help in any way they could. The talk began, but communication didn't, and it took an Ethiopian who had lived in the U.S. for many years to spot the difficulty.

"The Ethiopian came to ask for specific things, and the Americans were glad to assist, but the two sides couldn't communicate. For the Ethiopian didn't say that he wanted help, even though that's what he had come for; he couldn't make it explicit. He quoted the Bible to the effect that if one has good things, he should share them; he was very implicit. Both sides were lost," this man said.

"For the American is very explicit; he wants a 'yes' or 'no.' If someone tries to speak figuratively, the American is confused. Yet Ethiopians always imply. It's difficult for us to say what we want clearly," he added.

"Ethiopians are ambiguous. You can say something that can be interpreted 101 ways. Even when people say something which seems straight, inside there are double meanings," commented a young Ethiopian woman.

This cautious, indirect approach is perhaps one aspect of a more general sense of suspicion which a series of unfortunate contacts with foreign powers has deeply implanted in the Ethiopian character. Whether it was Portuguese missionaries or Italian troops, these influences have been destructive. Thus the not illogical question that an Ethiopian asks himself on the arrival of an outsider: "Is he going to make war or try to convert me?"

"It is a suspicion, not a hatred. Our rulers have always said that we must guard ourselves against foreigners. It's not an antagonism or resentment; we really don't have enemies. But even in his dealings with another African — or even a fellow countryman — an Ethiopian will guard himself. With Europeans, it's worse. It takes time, but an Ethiopian can become as close a friend as anybody," one man said.

"In Ethiopia it takes a long time to know a person and an even longer time to lose a friendship; in the U.S. it is just the opposite," added another man.

Lurking behind many of the misunderstandings between Ethiopians and Americans is the community orientation of the former and the individual orientation of the latter.

"All interpersonal problems — how close you can become, what you can expect, whether you can trust — are related to this issue," said one Ethiopian, who pointed out that an American seems to preserve for himself certain freedoms which tend to fence him off from other people.

"Trying to establish an interpersonal relationship in the U.S. is like trying to negotiate over or break down that fence; it is almost like a series of concentric circles. You have to break down different levels before you become friends," he said.

"American society is very competitive, whereas outside of the cities in Ethiopia there is much more cooperation than competition. In the U.S. the individual is the center of activity. In Ethiopia the individual has the necessary freedom to act, but always at the back of his mind is the interest of the larger society — the tribe, the clan, or the whole country," added another man.

An Ethiopian whose first stop in the U.S. was New York City was stunned by the lonely crowd atmosphere.

"Everybody was physically close but distant. There was no personal contact of any sort," she said.

"People are very much in a hurry; they're not standing on the street greeting and chatting. Everybody is rushing to go somewhere; it's very businesslike. People don't seem to have a lot of time for each other," noted an Ethiopian.

"In the U.S. time is a mechanical thing, a commodity. For an Ethiopian, time is morning or afternoon; it's not compartmentalized," added another man.

The American's warm but hurried greeting appears abrupt to the more leisurely Ethiopians, whose encounters involve a long series of questions and an offer of food and drink.

"If someone comes to your house at any time of day, you must offer food, even if you have just finished lunch," explained an Ethiopian woman.

"The traditional Ethiopian finds it offensive when an American just says "Hello' and gives him a pat on the back. It seems too slight and informal; it rubs him the wrong way until he understands the different custom," mentioned one Ethiopian who has lived for some time in the U.S.

Particularly puzzling to a newly arrived Ethiopian is the way that he will be suddenly left alone after a cordial welcome.

"In Ethiopia when a new person comes to a city, the hosts tend to stick with him – not leave him in a hotel but rather invite him to their home. They want to be around him and feel they cannot leave him alone. If an American attempts to pay for such lodging, however, it appears rude. Thus it might seem impolite to an American for an Ethiopian *not* to offer to pay when he stays in an American home," one Ethiopian said.

People shake hands more in Ethiopia, and both men and women rise when a newcomer enters the room. "If I meet a person for the second time in the same hour, I would still shake his hand," said an Ethiopian executive.

The reluctance shown by Americans of the same sex to embrace or hold hands appears unduly restrained to the more effusive Ethiopians, who feel that such signs of affection show a closeness without implying any sexual interest.

"If we act this way in the U.S., it will be misunderstood as homosexuality," said one Ethiopian, who told how an emotional airport sendoff drew head-turning gawks from incredulous Americans.

An Ethiopian college student was dumbfounded when she returned to her American campus following the three-month summer break.

"My roommate only said, 'Hi! How are you?' She didn't even shake hands. When we salute each other – particularly after such a long time – we would kiss and embrace," she said.

Yet a girl and boy holding hands – conduct taken for granted by Americans – would be considered highly improper in many Ethiopian villages.

The communal approach engendered by the extended family is reflected in the fact that any relative is considered a brother or sister. This feeling of mutual concern extends to acquaintances as well, and social law dictates that one should visit a person in the hospital, even if it is only the friend of a relative. The close-knit family bonds are drawn even tighter at the time of a christening, wedding, or funeral.

Traditionally, Ethiopians who lost a relative would visit the family for at least seven days. Urbanization is complicating this practice, but employees are still generally allowed three days off to stay with the bereaved in-laws.

"The people all sleep together, as many as the house will hold. This is shocking to foreigners, but it is normal to us," said one Ethiopian woman, who added that there was no adequate translation of "privacy" in Amharic.

"When one says 'privacy,' I think of loneliness," she said. "If an Ethiopian student rents an apartment in the U.S., it seems as if hundreds of people are always going in and out. Americans don't understand this, and they think we are not being considerate of the owner. We look at it from a different angle; we like to have people around us."

"In my house there was one bedroom for all the children — my brother, two cousins, a little sister, and me. We were all huddled together in two beds," added another young woman.

"In Ethiopia everything you have is shared. At the dinner table each person takes a piece of bread and helps himself to the food in the center," she added.

"It is difficult for an Ethiopian to stay by himself like this, and it is especially difficult to eat alone," according to an Ethiopian student who rents an efficiency apartment in the U.S. The deeply ingrained communal pattern is even carried over to U.S. restaurants, where Ethiopians may startle Americans by sharing the same hamburger.

If an Ethiopian student adjusts too well to American self-sufficiency, however, he runs the risk of alienating friends from his own country, who feel that he is ignoring them. Yet even in Ethiopia, urbanization has contributed to an emphasis on the needs of the immediate family and a consequent neglect of some of the long-standing social obligations.

One American custom that many Ethiopians appreciate but find difficult to adopt is calling people by their first names. "It is still difficult for me, even after six years, to call someone — especially an older person — by his first name. I prefer your way, but I can't get used to it," said one Ethiopian.

Dramatic differences in the traditional educational patterns of the two countries have led to problems for American Peace Corps volunteers teaching in Ethiopia.

"They were unpopular for some time because their methods seemed too simple. Ethiopian students were expecting someone who dictates. When the American teacher tried to discuss things, to get the students to participate, they felt he was not a good teacher," explained a prospective Ethiopian teacher currently studying in the U.S.

"I now have my own philosophy of education, which is a product of the two cultures. I will not reproduce the American system, but I will reflect it. Nor will I reproduce the Ethiopian way; it will be a synthesis. I want to help the individual to explore his own potential," he added.

Accustomed to treating the teacher with the utmost respect at home, Ethiopians are initially stunned by the seeming indifference students show towards their professors and the general informality of an American classroom. An Ethiopian who recently earned his Ph.D. in the U.S. told how his first day in an American university almost ended his overseas educational experience.

"Students were sitting with their feet up on the desks, nobody got up when the teacher came in, and then he started out by telling a dirty joke. I asked myself, 'What did I come here for? Is this the way I am going to get an education?'

"The Ethiopian initially interprets this informality as laxness or immorality. Rather it is just to ease the tension. It takes time to get used to it," he added.

"In the U.S. the student is asked to interpret; in Ethiopia, to reproduce. The teacher puts something on the board, and you memorize it," said an Ethiopian student, who still recalls how failure to properly prepare her Amharic lesson cost her a slap with a ruler many years ago.

Another Ethiopian was strongly critical of this approach. "If there is fear, I don't think you can learn anything. In the U.S. a student may be clipping his fingernails, but he's listening. In Ethiopia we say, 'Sit properly,' but don't care how much the student learns."

An older Ethiopian, however, was more concerned that this discipline was breaking down and felt that "a change for the worse" was taking place in that students no longer showed the proper respect for their teachers. "We emulated the teacher; we wanted to be like him," he said somewhat nostalgically.

There appears to be some difference of opinion as to how much the traditional Ethiopian pattern is changing. One man felt that the teacher-student relationship has lost some of its authoritarian nature and now closely parallels the U.S. style. Another maintained that "strict reliance on punishment to get lessons across" has by no means disappeared.

One Western import which has clearly left its imprint on urban Ethiopians is the custom of dating, even though tradition-minded parents view it with disfavor. Whereas the American mother will be concerned if her daughter does *not* go out, the Ethiopian mother will worry if her daughter does. "It is more discreet; you sneak out," said one young woman.

"There's a lot of hiding. You say that you are going to your girl friend's house and instead meet a boy," added another woman.

"For the traditional Ethiopian mother — who did not date herself and had an arranged marriage — it's a very exotic thing for her daughter to go out," one man said.

"A teenage girl cannot tell her father she is going out with a man; he wouldn't allow it. But this doesn't mean it doesn't happen," added an Ethiopian father. "He thinks of his daughter as an untouchable jewel who needs protection and insulation from a bad world. He doesn't view it as denying her rights."

Unlike her American counterpart, an Ethiopian girl who dates many boys will find that her fickle heart hurts her chances of finding a husband. "The idea that a woman can date you today and another man next week is really shocking. She is expected to stick to one man," according to an Ethiopian male.

The anonymity which a large city like Addis Ababa might seem to provide for multiple dating is illusory, for there is a class of people that move in the same circles. "They know each other very well," one man said.

As household organizer, the woman is responsible for managing the maids and often the family finances, caring for the children, and — in the countryside — working in the fields. "She is the budget officer, so to speak, and the husband is the chief executive," was the way one Ethiopian summed it up.

Another man felt that there is a more egalitarian relationship and consequently greater mutual respect between working class husbands and wives than among the nobility, where women were exchanged to establish family relationships.

A third man seemed to downplay this distinction. "In Ethiopian culture women of all classes have fared well; they are very important," he said.

The question of women's rights outside the home led to varying views from an Ethiopian man and woman.

"If a woman is educated, there will be no discrimination in terms of job opportunities and payment. The problem is education. Every farmer wants his son to be as highly educated as possible, but he says that third grade is good enough for his daughter. A women's movement in Ethiopia would have to convince parents that education was good for their daughters," said the man, who cited the presence of female army officers, politicians, and even a deputy foreign minister as evidence of equality once the all-important education has been attained.

Not so, according to the woman, who maintained that education alone would not ensure equal treatment. "A woman is still stereotyped as a secretary or chosen for her looks and not for her brains. She may be asked for a date to get a job; this is degrading," she said. Working against women's equality, in her opinion, were the legal concept of man as master of the house and the religious notion of woman as the cause of evil.

Some support was given this position by an Ethiopian male, who claimed that the biggest problem for Ethiopian men in dealing with American women was treating them as complete intellectual equals.

"In their society women are supposed to be submissive and obedient; they are there only to do favors for men. With this kind of orientation, they don't know how to relate to women as intellectual equals. Maintaining an image of male dominance for the most part does not work in the U.S., but they think that because their women are impressed, American women will be," he said.

While Ethiopians tend to agree that service is polite and personal in their country and brusque and businesslike in the U.S., they differ as to the precise relationship between the one performing the service and the one being waited on in the two societies. One Ethiopian, for example, characterized the relationship in the U.S. as one of "mutual respect"; another termed it "mutual contempt."

"People in the service occupations in Ethiopia are extremely polite — to the extent that a person like me might not like. They are very submissive; it almost appears like servitude. In the U.S. the waiter is very busy; he almost throws things at you. Even though he hopes to receive a tip, he still appears standoffish," one man said.

The benefits of the more cordial Ethiopian approach were extolled by another man. "The person being waited on looks at the service person with respect and friendship. If you go to a restaurant often, you will know him on a first-name basis. You can become good friends. In the U.S., it is always a rush; it's difficult to establish such a friendship," he said.

Yet another Ethiopian cast a negative light on this apparently positive picture. "The servant or waiter is expected to politely wait on the person. He has to take whatever the other person gives him — belittling, orders, insults. He accepts his role because of cultural conditioning. He has been enslaved; he can't do otherwise," this man said.

"In Ethiopia only the servants serve; manual work is not dignified. In the U.S. the person serving does not feel inferior; the important thing is how much money he will make. It's just a job to him. In Ethiopia, it's important what *kind* of work you do," according to another man.

The need to perform menial tasks to help finance an American education can come as a rude jolt to the newly arrived.

"Mopping floors is very difficult for Ethiopian students, especially after having been considered respected college students at home," one man commented.

Yet many students, burying their pride, work part-time as waiters or bellboys and still manage to compile enviable academic records. "Some of these people are doing a fantastic job," said one Ethiopian graduate student who had researched students' adjustment to U.S. life.

Not making that job any easier is their immediate immersion in a racial milieu whose agonies and nuances — bedeviling enough to Americans who have grown up with them — are particularly perplexing to those from a society where people are not seen as black and white.

"I used to think of myself as a human being. Then all of a sudden somebody tells me I'm black," said one young woman who attended college in the U.S. "I used to consider Americans as Americans, but my schoolmates said 'blacks' and 'whites,' so I adopted these terms."

"That's precisely the point; there's no concept of color at home. Racism has not been a problem for us historically. The white man did not come as a master, though Italy tried for five years. Ethiopians don't hate the white man because he is white. Relationships are personal, not racial," added a man studying in the U.S.

Categorized as a "black" while he is in the U.S., the Ethiopian must necessarily empathize with the position of the black American.

"He is my situational friend. This affects my feelings towards whites," said one Ethiopian, who later told how an acquaintance, on being denied admittance to a party, went home, changed from Western to African attire, and was readily let in.

Further problems arise in Ethiopians' relations with black Americans, due in part to the differing interpretations of Emperor Haile Selassie's statement nearly 20 years ago that Ethiopians did not consider themselves Negroes. Some American blacks took this to mean that Ethiopians — unlike other Africans — did not consider themselves black people. Many Ethiopians, however, insist that his comment was misinterpreted.

" 'Negro' to him meant being enslaved, and we had pride in our being independent," explained one Ethiopian woman.

The whole complicated racial picture was brought into sharper focus by a perceptive Ethiopian student.

"I keep my mind open, but for many Ethiopians it is very difficult. They come with a generalized preconception of racial strife. This difficulty is compounded by expecting friendship from American blacks. Yet the blacks tend to identify more with the West than with Africa. There is also a false pride among some Ethiopians that we are unique and different from the rest of Africa. If you come with this feeling, you expect to be accepted by the Caucasians because you are Semitic," he said.

Expecting to find the streets paved with gold, Ethiopians are shocked by the presence of poverty in the U.S. and the budget-mindedness of most Americans. Equally surprising is the large number of Sunday churchgoers, for Hollywood movies have created the distinct impression that religion has long been left behind. The much-discussed American materialism, however, readily fulfills Ethiopian expectations.

"The American is always on the go — working night and day. He has to make money. The enjoyment he gets out of accomplishment is material; he has to have a TV and a car at an early age. Yet he never relaxes to enjoy what he is getting. For after working hard all day, if he wants to watch TV, he will fall asleep," said one woman.

Yet another Ethiopian made the point that "fascination with material things is not uniquely American" and expressed concern that many young Ethiopians — beguiled by American popular culture — never scratch the surface when it comes to understanding the inner workings of U.S. society.

"The roots of American attitudes are found in the political process, the press, the judiciary, and the economic system. These are the foundations of the culture. But students respond quickly to the popular culture, to the music. They have fabulous stereo record players and James Brown (a popular singer) records; a car is also important. But these things, for sure, are not the dynamics of American civilization," he said.

"We are trying to arrange a marriage between the Western way and our own way and make something out of it that will reflect genuine Ethiopian customs, rather than taking lock, stock, and barrel from abroad. This is true of dating, the political process, the economy — everything," added another man.

There must be a two-way educational exchange, however, if Ethiopians are to help dispel the "jungle" stereotype of Africa that many Americans still hold.

"I have been asked if I live in a hut or a cave, if I ever wore a shirt before coming to the U.S.," said one Ethiopian student, who told of a friend who had finally had enough of such questions. When asked where she lived, this girl replied, "At the top of a tall tree." "And how do you get up there?" persisted the gullible questioner. "We use elevators," she said.

9

JAMAICA

As she set foot inside her New York apartment for the first time, a five-year-old Jamaican girl sensed that something was amiss. For there was no veranda, no sense of being connected with the out-of-doors, only the prison-like appearance of the confining four walls. She turned to her mother and said, "This house isn't finished yet."

Accustomed to the open spaces and trees of his tropical environment, the Jamaican experiences immediate claustrophobia when confronted with the towering, compressed landscape of an American inner city.

"The walls keep closing in on you. If you locked a Jamaican in a room for a month, he would die, so intense is the feeling of physical isolation and removal from his friends," according to a Jamaican who has lived for many years in the U.S.

Equally unusual to the recent arrival is the tremendous organization and specialization which permeates American life.

"Everything requires paperwork − credit cards, a social security card. Even students have to travel with a lot of paper. In Jamaica only the man who drives a car has a piece of paper," one man said.

Another striking aspect of the American scene is the way in which pockets of poverty can be conveniently tucked away in the hidden corners of an essentially affluent society.

"In the U.S. you can go about your business very easily and not be aware of broken-down houses. In Jamaica every posh residential area has a fringe of substandard housing that one has to drive through to get to the good houses. One needn't be aware of urban poverty in the U.S. if he avoids certain streets," this man added.

Gaining an understanding of American institutions is not made any easier by the seemingly perpetual changes they undergo.

"It's a most dynamic thing − this continuous mutation. Every day there is a change of something. You have to be as fast as light to keep up with it," said one Jamaican, who has found the U.S. a parochial as well as a powerful country.

"My classmates thought that I wore grass skirts and lived in a tree. I went along and told them that my father and mother lived in different branches. There's this 'banana boat' stereotype," added a Jamaican woman who had studied at an American university.

While visions of banana boats blur the American's perception, Jamaicans suffer from another malady which distorts their image of life in the U.S. One Jamaican has called this the "Hollywood psychosis – an exaggerated concept of the U.S. in which no one is in need of anything."

Led to believe that the U.S. has the most, best, and greatest of everything and that almost every American is a potential millionaire, the Jamaican views the U.S. as did the European immigrant at the turn of the century who believed that he could coin money if he just worked hard enough.

Some Jamaicans do in fact earn 10 to 15 times what they made in Jamaica and return home with what seems a vast amount of money.

"While in the U.S., the Jamaican worker will save most of his salary, shop in Murphy's basement instead of Garfinckel's, and return 5 to 10 years later as a rich man – comparatively. You can't tell people back there that America isn't heaven when Carey Jones can go back and buy the whole neighborhood," said one Jamaican who has helped many fellow countrymen adjust to life in the U.S.

"Yet a Jamaican who comes to the U.S. without skills might think of suicide; he would be so frustrated. He dreamed of utopia only to find that he can scarcely buy a meal," this man added.

"I'm a student; I stay flat broke all of the time," commented a young man. "Yet if I went home, people would expect me to bring gifts. It would be unbelievable that I wouldn't have American dollar bills and clothes to give away."

The image of the affluent American has been firmly entrenched in the Jamaican mind by waves of wealthy tourists, whose generally ostentatious manner has not exactly endeared them to struggling Jamaicans. Yet this stereotype is being shattered by the increasing number of young impecunious Americans – packs strapped across their backs – traipsing across Jamaica looking for places to camp.

"This is bringing about a warmer association. These young people get along with the Jamaicans on a much more friendly basis," noted one Jamaican.

"The American is seen as brash, loud-talking, and materialistic — less concerned with spiritual values. Thus there is trepidation on the part of relatives when a Jamaican goes to live in the U.S. that he will lose his softness, kindness, and humaneness. But most of us find that Americans are more pleasant to live among than we had thought; we are pleasantly surprised," a Jamaican student said.

Americans can startle Jamaicans, however, with discussions of personal matters in hotel lobbies or supermarkets rather than in drawing rooms, where Jamaicans feel such subjects belong.

"An American might talk loudly about her husband's coming down with a hernia or a friend's miscarriage. I wilt at that sort of thing. Yet Americans don't yell at each other in the street; our people are tougher on each other," one Jamaican said.

A sharp distinction must be drawn, in this man's view, between urban and rural Jamaicans, for the former have fallen victims to the more impersonal, less hospitable world of the city.

"I want to shy away from the 'noble savage' image, but the rural Jamaican is a fantastic person. This is where Jamaican hospitality began. A visitor has to partake of their hospitality, to share some food, even if it is just a little," he said.

"The idea of community is very strong in the rural area. People help each other, are concerned about each other. A baby born in Kingston will often be sent back to relatives in the rural area," he continued.

Coming from a society where the extended family is the norm, Jamaicans are initially disturbed by the impersonal aspect of life in the U.S. Accustomed to the community feeling engendered by life in a boarding school, a Jamaican student soon senses this lack of group spirit in a big city American university.

"People are friends in the classrooms, and that's it," said one former student, who nonetheless appreciated the vibrant intellectual atmosphere in her new setting.

"It takes a long time to feel part of the wider society in the U.S. Americans tend to exclude you in discussions. There's the feeling that 'You're a foreigner, so you wouldn't understand,' " she said.

For one raised to the exacting standards of proper British etiquette, however, the impersonal side of American life can come as a welcome relief from lifelong restraints. "I like the anonymity of being in the U.S., of standing on a street corner where nobody knows who you are," one

Jamaican said.

Because Jamaicans do not draw as sharp a line between work and social relationships as do Americans, the newly arrived Jamaican often feels rebuffed by the indifference of an American co-worker or neighbor, who may prefer to choose his friends on grounds other than proximity.

Even more distressing is what Jamaicans view as an overly reciprocal approach to friendship on the part of Americans.

"In Jamaica if somebody likes you and does something for you, this is an act that cannot be paid for. Thus it is a strange concept to the Jamaican when an American says, 'So and so *owes* me a favor.' If a Jamaican invites you to stay in his house, nothing could be more upsetting than for you to offer money," explained a Jamaican educator.

Nearly every Jamaican can tell of being asked to accompany an American to a cafeteria lunch and then being left behind to pay his own bill — a victim of the much misunderstood American "Dutch treat" custom.

"This is bad enough when it happens to a man, but it's even worse for a woman. For when a man says, 'Come and join us for lunch,' she never has any doubt that he will pay. Then all of a sudden she is told, 'You owe $2.25,' " one Jamaican said.

"Some Americans will discuss the check — down to the last cent — in the presence of everybody. They will quibble over who had beer and who didn't have beer. This is very distasteful to us," added a Jamaican woman.

Equally unappetizing is the way in which an American taxi driver or policeman will snap back an answer in a manner considered highly rude in Jamaica.

"When I was in New York for the first time, I had trouble making out the numbers of the tall buildings," one Jamaican said. "So I asked the taxi driver, 'Is this 1062?'; and he answered, 'Can't you read?' "

"Once I heard a little old lady ask a policeman if there was going to be a parade. He shot back, 'Whadaya think, lady?' I couldn't imagine any of our police speaking like that," added another Jamaican.

Yet some Jamaicans come to acknowledge an efficiency — however abrasive — among Americans working in service jobs.

"At first at American lunch counters I would wait for the waitress to smile at me and ask for my order in a polite, leisurely way; she was waiting for me to yell out my order. The American way is more efficient, for the waitress can polish the counter and take an order at the same time. The

Jamaican waitress has to polish first and then take the order," said a Jamaican student.

"The waitress in the U.S. doesn't feel inferior — which she isn't — to the guy ordering the food. In Jamaica, people in these jobs are constantly on the defensive or totally servile. People who sell things in stores are rude to other Jamaicans, though they might not be rude to tourists. It's like an insult to them if I come in to buy something," added another student.

This increased surliness on the part of Jamaican service people and the heightened resentment towards customers — particularly wealthy fellow countrymen — is a relatively recent development, according to one Jamaican. In the past, she maintained, relations between served and serving were marked by mutual courtesy.

"The Jamaican being waited on can be arrogant, haughty, and a little condescending — sometimes more than a little," added a Jamaican woman. "Service people in Jamaica would often rather work with Americans and British than with a fellow Jamaican."

"In Jamaica there is still a stigma on the person who is doing the serving. In the U.S. nobody feels shame or embarrassment about menial labor; it's just a job. A Jamaican will do work in the U.S. that he would never do back home. This is not just because he is over here and anonymous but because his attitude changes," noted another woman, who later referred to an article in an American magazine on the incomes of various occupations, including truck driver. "In a Jamaican magazine, the truck driver wouldn't have been considered. He wouldn't want to be mentioned, and nobody else would be interested," she said.

This attitude, of course, hits at the very heart of the entire question of hierarchy in Jamaica and whether or not status is losing its traditional hold on the social structure.

"There is a feeling of hierarchy among the rich and those who control the jobs, but only *they* have this feeling. The masses don't regard them as aristocrats. It's a one-way street. In the old days of the colonial hierarchy the manners were distinctly British. These were imitated by those on the make, the social climbers," explained one Jamaican.

"There were always people one didn't associate too closely with, though this wasn't explicit. A boy developed a violent crush on me when I was 12 years old, and my mother was terribly upset that *that* person — someone out of our sphere — had the effrontery to do so," commented a young woman.

"This had everything to do with family, whether one was well-bred or not — not with material possessions. The feeling was not one of 'them and us' but rather of 'decent and not-quite-so-decent.' Young people see this as artificial and want to break it down. Older people see it as commendable, that it is the natural order of things to have good people as friends," she added.

Traditional Jamaicans can thus undergo what one termed "status disequilibrium" when they arrive in the U.S.

"It is shocking to come from a privileged position and have to work as a janitor or taxi driver. If a Jamaican has to do it to survive, he will. But he will constantly reminisce about how his father was a teacher, much to the ridicule of his American co-workers. His perspective of himself becomes lessened. I'm glad it happens," confessed a student in favor of eliminating class barriers.

"The British influence is still strong, though we like to say we're shedding it. But if you turn around and look at our customs and habits, they're still predominantly British. We talk a lot about our African heritage now; we're almost flagellating ourselves to be more African, to see if we can't wipe out the British tradition," one woman observed.

Several Jamaicans attributed the strong feeling of family and community — particularly in the villages — to their African background. Love for music and dancing and considerable skill at both are also traced to African roots.

"There was no cohesive Africanism because our whole passage to the new world and our living on the plantations was too disjointed. But there have always been linkages with Africa, though it was never fashionable during our colonial past to say so," according to one young Jamaican woman, who felt that age was an important factor in determining where one looked for a cultural heritage.

"People in my parents' generation are more pro-British. Young people say that we have had enough influence from the British," she said.

Amidst discussions of African versus British background, one should not overlook, however, the uniquely Jamaican component, which has served to temper the traits of the islanders' alien ancestry. One Jamaican described this ingredient as an "easygoingness — a relaxed, mellow attitude toward life."

"Jamaicans don't worry about tomorrow; they just live for today. They're not bound up in terrible emotions like Americans," was the explanation given by another Jamaican.

This mellow mood can harden into militancy, however, for the Jamaican who feels that he has been discriminated against in the United States. The picture most Jamaicans paint of race relations in the U.S. is, unfortunately, not a pleasant one. From the older Jamaican who has never gotten over the shock of the small letter "c" (for "colored") in a church directory 30 years ago to the student who is convinced that institutionalized racism persists, the spectre of racial prejudice continues to mar the Jamaican's overall American experience.

"I came to the U.S. in the mid-1960's — a time of civil rights activism. Although people said that gains were being made, it didn't seem that way to me," said one Jamaican, then a student. "I was looking for a new place to stay and knocked on the door of a house that advertised rooms for rent. The white woman who came to the door was so obviously shocked that I gave her my educational background to assure her that I wasn't coming to rob her. She said, 'This is a *white* house' and later insisted that the room had been taken. I said, 'If that's the case, you'd better take the sign out of the window.' "

Though she was convinced that a basic institutionalized racism would linger "forever and aye," this Jamaican has found that a positive approach to people on an individual basis can cut through surface prejudices. "Then you will be reasonably well accepted," she said.

"The Jamaican is not unprepared for racial problems in the U.S., but he often prefers to ignore them because his chief aim is to make money," added another Jamaican.

The agonizing issue of race has also complicated Jamaicans' relations with American blacks, partly because Jamaicans absorbed white American attitudes and partly because they themselves felt, as one Jamaican put it, "schizophrenic" about race.

"Jamaicans tried to see themselves as not black because black behavior was defined in a certain (negative) way. One Jamaican woman was traumatized to find that she was not accepted in Britain after trying her whole life to say that she was not black in terms of manners," said a Jamaican who had lived in England.

"Jamaicans did look down on American blacks. This was particularly true 20 years ago, and it was based on ignorance. Black Americans often felt that West Indians in general were arrogant and unsympathetic," one man said.

"The American black felt that the Jamaican's style was different — that he was acting like 'Whitey,' " added a long-time resident in the United States.

"Now Jamaicans feel more at home with American blacks. There's a general feeling that the white American can never be sincere, that he tries too hard. This is based on the myth that blacks will never be accepted by whites," this woman continued.

"This is not my personal experience, however. I don't have that feeling; I have white friends," she was quick to add.

"Because of British colonization, my value system in some instances is closer to that of white Americans, but I feel more fraternity with blacks," commented a man who described himself as a lower-middle class Jamaican.

"Today the Jamaican empathizes more with the American black than formerly. There is a feeling that we never had before. The image of Martin Luther King, Jr., has done a lot," added another Jamaican.

Adjusting to American life involves more, however, than picking one's way through the thorny racial thicket. Nearly all Jamaicans, particularly males, view the U.S. as a female-oriented society; and a man who for more than a decade has helped Jamaicans in the U.S. resolve domestic difficulties has this advice for newly arrived men: "This is a woman's country. If you don't want to go to prison or the morgue too soon, you had better go along with the program."

"The idea of male supremacy is strong in Jamaica. Women have traditionally deferred to men in all areas and have waited on them hand and foot, though there is now some change. My father pretended not to know where the kitchen was; there is a lot of serving and spoiling men by their wives, and there is less sharing of housework than in an average American home. Yet the Jamaican woman doesn't try to get her husband to help with the kids and the housework. She is happier to accept her role," according to one young woman.

A Jamaican male, however, thought that was putting the case too strongly. "The woman is the center of the family structure, but neither women nor men dominate. In the U.S. the women dominate," said this man, who cited the recent case in which the wife of an American mayor spoke disparagingly of her husband in front of a group of newsmen.

Women's Liberation, according to another man, was important "up to a point"; that is, it was essential to have women more involved in roles outside the home, such as politics or social work. "But at home we want them to take care of the kids, keep the house clean and tidy, and see that there are enough groceries. That won't be changed," he concluded.

"Women's Lib supporters in Jamaica are the affluent types — the copy cats. They used to copy the English, now the Americans. Whatever appears in the newspapers, they leap at it," offered another man.

Equal time must be given, however, to a dissenting female voice, who felt that the day of male dominance had passed. "Women can have a dual role in Jamaica. Their place is no longer felt to be in the home, and this has evoked no antagonism from their male counterparts," she insisted. "Today more Jamaican women are working — for a better self-concept — even if they don't need the money."

Yet in urban, educated society a strong double standard seems to persist. "Dating is the rule among city dwellers, and girls in dating circles have less freedom than men. You're always under the eye of the family," said one young woman, who told how Jamaican men complained that Jamaican girls were fussier than British or American girls.

"A Jamaican girl will check out a man's credentials more. She wants to see him in the total context of family and educational background. Many Jamaican girls would rather sit at home than go out with the wrong people," she said.

A more open, less inhibited life style characterizes rural Jamaica. "The people there live very naturally. They can go for a walk in the moonlight or to the eternal beach to swim. There is a great deal of freedom for both boys and girls to move around — with no chaperon in the background," one man said.

Generally eschewing church weddings, rural dwellers consider a couple living together as validly married. "They have not accepted middle class European values; thus they don't view them as the norm," explained a Jamaican social scientist.

Nor have they allowed the clock to rule their lives. "Dawn is not at 6 o'clock; it's when the sun comes up. Punching the timeclock is not yet a part of the Jamaican character," another man said.

"In the U.S. if you are due at work at 9 o'clock, you come right at 9 and leave at 4:30, with half an hour for lunch. In Jamaica you might arrive at 9:30 and take an hour and a half for lunch but then stay until after 6 o'clock. If a man meets a friend while going to work, he might stop and have a drink with him before going on to work. But in the U.S., when one is on his way to work, nothing is going to stop him," said one Jamaican, who described the difficulties a fellow countryman had in adjusting to the tight American timetable.

"This man's boss told him that there would be a meeting from 11 to 12 and a second meeting at 12:15. A limousine would be waiting to take them to the second meeting at 12:01, which the Jamaican took as meaning 12:10 or so. At 11:59 he took a drink of soda. His boss was frantic because he kept the limo waiting 5 minutes and made them late for the next meeting," he said.

A story is told about a group of Englishmen who had some critical comments during their first few days in Jamaica. "These natives are lazy; look how slowly they walk," said one of the men. "After three months the Englishmen couldn't walk at all and had to go back to Newcastle. As a reaction to the tropical environment, we have developed a slower pace of life," added a Jamaican.

Attitudes toward work must be understood, moreover, in light of the colonial slavery system, in which, as one Jamaican expressed it, "Work was like a punishment; it was never associated with remuneration."

"When slavery was abolished in 1838, most people went to the backland, each to his own farm. They did not want to work on the sugar estate again unless they needed cash. From the estate owner's point of view, these small farmers were lazy, but they worked hard on their own land," added another man, who admired the never-give-up attitude of his rural countrymen.

"They keep on trying," he said proudly. "You can watch a man pushing a handcart over the hills for miles in the hot sun. He could lie down under the shade of a tree, but he doesn't. He keeps on pushing the cart."

10

IRAN

An official Iranian government publication declares, "It is in keeping with the national character that while seeking new solutions to age-old problems, the Iranians have found it necessary to profit from the traditions of an extraordinarily rich past. Thus life in Iran today is a happy mixture of the best of both worlds, a continuation of traditional values adapted when necessary to the requirements of modern society."

Perhaps foremost among the qualities that characterize the Iranian people are strong bonds of friendship, a careful respect for the honor and integrity of one's colleagues, and the maintenance of close and enduring family relationships. It is because of the strength of these values that the manner in which Iranians view the American life style offers particularly valuable insight into the fascinating panorama of intercultural relations.

The general American concept of friendship, which allows the word "friend" to be applied to acquaintances from virtually every aspect of one's past or present daily life without necessarily implying close ties or inseparable bonds, is often a puzzle for the Iranian.

Used to a more intense type of comradeship in his homeland, one Iranian exchange student declared emphatically, "Back in Iran a friend is a *friend*. You are like brothers and you stick together no matter what. It isn't a term to be used lightly, for one does not hesitate to help a friend in any area in which he needs assistance."

If such assistance should take the form of a loan, the student said, an Iranian would lend his friend the money without hesitation with his friend's word as the guarantee of repayment. The American aversion to loans among friends, as expressed in the saying, "Before borrowing money from a friend decide what you need more," is especially foreign to the Iranian, who sees mutual dependence and trust as the very basis of friendship. The idea of a friend asking another to sign a note for a small loan, much less charging interest on the money, would seem insulting to the Iranian.

"Where is friendship," asked one student, "if I must sign documents as if at a bank?" An explanation that the American simply wished to assure payment of the debt in case of the death of his friend simply increased the misunderstanding. "Had the situation been reversed," the student declared, "the thought of being deprived of my friend's presence would cause so much sorrow that I could not be so calculating as to plan in advance how to recover the money in event of tragedy."

Trust in one's colleagues is very basic to the Iranian relationship. An Iranian rug dealer who had lived in the United States for years told of how a childhood friend had brought over a consignment of rugs and was ready to give the merchandise to acquaintances of the U.S. resident on approval without securing receipts for the rugs.

"I told him that you couldn't do that here, that the Americans would think him crazy or be afraid to take the rugs. Still, I could never bring him to issue the documents because such behavior in Iran would insult the other man's integrity.

"The United States is a very formal society. In Iran we have, I think, a more informal friendship-type society. The public credit checks that an American accepts as customary when making a purchase would, at first, be humiliating to an Iranian."

The American's reluctance to become emotionally involved with other individuals he calls friends and the compartmentalization of relationships as "friends from work," "friends from school," "friends from home" often appear cold and formal to the Iranian. A woman who had lived in the United States for five years, commenting on the casualness and impermanence of U.S. relationships, said, "Here you can feel 'liked' by many people but never sure of your acceptance the next day."

"Isn't it amazing," said another longtime resident, "that you work with a person for 10 months, consider him your friend, and then he leaves for another position, and you never hear a word from him. To us this is very shocking, and we can't consider these people friends when we meet them again."

Taking time to talk with one's friends, to listen to their ideas and thus continually keep the relationships strong, is inherently important in Iranian society. Although the pace of life in industrializing Tehran and other large cities of Iran has made some inroads on the time available for such courtesies, Iranians take pride in their concern for other people.

One girl spoke about an instance where an American friend came to town after an absence of several months. "I had a tremendous amount of work that had to be completed by the next day, but I couldn't tell my friend I had no time to see her. So I suggested that we meet for a two-hour lunch. Well, we talked for four hours, and I had to stay up to finish my project, but how could I do otherwise?"

The welcome manifested toward friends during chance meetings is even more apparent during a friend's visit to one's home. "Here one must make a telephone call first to ask permission to come over. If you arrive unexpectedly, the American friend will be surprised and might even ask you what you want," observed one man.

"In Iran we receive friends at any time; they are always welcome. If someone drops in to visit, you attempt to have him eat something. And it would be an insult to the host to refuse."

A girl said, "It's an embarrassing situation for us to arrive at someone's home when they are eating and not be asked to join them. In my country, if my aunt stopped by, whatever I was eating I would share with her."

In the more formal occasions of home hospitality, the Iranians offer a lavish demonstration of the guest's welcome. Noting that "in the West, a man will not go beyond his means for hospitality, and that in Iran a person will, if necessary, go into debt for such a purpose," one man pointed out that a *mehman* or "guest" also is considered by Iranians as a "gift of God."

The strong Protestant ethic and the guilt that Americans feel if they take time from their work to engage in such activity as talking with acquaintances about non-work-related subjects is disconcerting to an Iranian. Although people from the two different cultures might agree with Benjamin Franklin's admonition, "Do you love life? Then do not squander time, for that is the stuff life is made of," an Iranian does not feel that talking with a friend is squandering time.

"Here," observed a professional man, "time is sold. It is your duty to work and one misses the opportunity to talk with friends."

Another noted, "People in the United States do not linger after classes, don't take time to speak with others. There is a 9 to 5 attitude of working that relegates casual conversation to after-office hours. The same person who continues to glance nervously at his work while you comment on some current event is an entirely different person at a party in the evening. He feels free of his duty to produce. We Iranians get our work done but are not so driven by a timetable. We don't divide our lives into segments."

A professional interpreter observed, "In Iran people have time for each other, even the dairyman, the mailman, the grocer. We speak to him about his family, his babies, his health, how business is going, and we *really* care."

This interest in others can lead to a very broad range of knowledge beyond one's particular area of expertise. A woman, noting that her father's business requires him to travel from city to city in Iran, said that he can tell at any given moment what is happening in the country and what people think about a particular subject. Such knowledge is not a result of a concentrated effort on her father's part, she said, but merely a result of being ready to talk with people beyond immediate business issues.

A grocer in Iran, affirmed a student, knows more about community life than his counterpart in the United States, because he is always speaking with his customers and learning from their experiences.

Coming from a more relaxed society where people "cry with your sadness and laugh with your gaiety," the Iranians are at first uncomfortable with the personal detachment of the Americans. Even the phrase, "How are you doing?" — which to an American is merely a pro forma greeting for which no reply but "Fine" is expected — can cause difficulties. The American is embarrassed by any more than a perfunctory reply and, until he becomes accustomed to the meaninglessness of the greeting, an Iranian may well be hurt by the lack of interest of his friends.

A man with years of residence in the United States said he rarely met someone who responded to a "How are you?" greeting with something of substance. He remembers with affection the reply of one older American office receptionist who answered his query, "How are you today?" She retorted, "How am I today? With such cold rainy weather and my arthritic condition how should I be? I feel terrible." Although the Iranian found such frankness a pleasant change, he noted with bemusement that all the other Americans at the office thought she was "crazy."

The American's acute consciousness of privacy of others and his ingrained reserve toward offering unsolicited help ("meddling in other people's affairs") can appear unfeeling to someone from a country such as Iran, where the interdependence of people is accepted and welcomed.

According to a man who sometimes counsels Iranian students in the United States, the newly arrived student is often struck by this difference in behavior during his first moments in the country. If someone, especially a foreigner, appeared confused in an Iranian airport, people would stop and offer assistance. The Americans, he observed, while they usually readily render assistance if asked, will refrain from embarrassing themselves by offering assistance to someone whom they think may prefer to solve his own problems.

Regional differences among Americans, with the most formal style of interpersonal relationships practiced on the east coast and more uninhibited patterns practiced in the Midwest, the South, and the West, make non-east coast locations favorites of the Iranians.

One girl, voicing her belief that first impressions are very important, said that the ideal situation would be for international visitors to avoid the northeastern part of the United States until later in the stay in order to first learn about the warmer aspects of the American personality in the Midwest or West. Another said the people from the South and from California are not "so stuffy and have time to talk with people."

The ability to get right to the point of an issue, a quality prized by Americans, can under certain circumstances be offensive to an Iranian used to achieving his goals through a subtle, indirect route.

The quality of *abru,* which translated literally means "color of one's face" and signifies such intangibles as one's prestige and reputation, makes the tactics of indirection rather than face-to-face confrontation important to the Iranian.

"A student told me, with rage in his voice, that his American professor had treated him shamelessly," began one account of abuse of *abru.* "I asked him why, and he said that the professor had observed that he was having trouble understanding the lecture. The instructor had asked the student publicly if he understood the content of the lecture. When he was informed that the student was having difficulty, the American professor said, 'Then, sir, I think that perhaps you should leave my class and better occupy your time elsewhere.' "

The student characterized as "shameless" the manner in which the American teacher suggested that the student improve his vocabulary before tackling the course. The American professor, on the other hand, unfamiliar with the importance of the Iranian concept of reputation, did not understand that his frank observation would be interpreted as a personal attack.

A middle-aged man, remembering his student days in the United States, noted that he once turned in an excellent paper a day late despite the professor's warning that late papers would be marked down a grade. He recalled how angry he was when the professor, when handing the paper back, told the class that "Mr. _____ turned in an 'A' paper, but because it was late in arrival it has received a grade of 'B.' " Unlike the average American student, the young Iranian was not angry so much at receiving the lower grade but at the particular act of the professor of announcing it openly to the class.

Pointing out that the professor could have achieved the same type of warning to the student without bringing about a direct public confrontation, one Iranian told a fable of an ancient king who had an ominous dream. In the dream the king saw himself aged and afflicted, with decaying and falling teeth. Calling together his court astrologers for an interpretation, the shaken king heard the first say, "Your Majesty, I regret to tell you that the interpretation must be bad. The dream means that you will die within a year." In a rage the king threw the brash astrologer out of his court and turned to the second man.

The second astrologer said, "Your Majesty, it is good news, the very best. It means that all your programs and projects will live on after you, and all your sons and daughters will survive you." The king, who was old and knew he might die soon, nevertheless was pleased with this interpretation and richly rewarded the astrologer.

The way truth can be spoken in different cultures and the importance of one's self image can offer problems for a person not alert to different national patterns of behavior.

"We never like to reveal our weaknesses," noted one Iranian. Another said that in attempting to avoid revealing his faults a student will make up a logical excuse if his work is not complete and feel completely justified in doing so. In Iran the professors expect such excuses and act accordingly. In the United States, on the other hand, a professor often loses all trust in the student if he first accepts an excuse and then learns that it is not true.

Similarly a professor who allows himself to be treated without the utmost respect or one who confesses ignorance on a subject is not generally taken seriously by Iranian students.

"The average student," said one man, "loses respect for a teacher when he is too friendly and common with the pupils. The teacher is considered a venerable gentleman. We are, at first, shocked at the casual atmosphere in the American classroom. Until he becomes accustomed to the differences, an Iranian will listen but not learn from such a professor. He sees him as an entertainer, an actor, not a teacher."

"The first time," another recounted, "my professor said to me, 'I don't know the answer; I will have to look it up,' I was shocked. I asked myself, 'Why is he teaching me?' In Iran he would give a wrong answer rather than admit ignorance. If not, he would lose all his *abru* in front of the students."

Outside the classroom, the indirect manner of achieving end results is continually resorted to in order to avoid unpleasant confrontation or open criticism.

"If I was sure that a certain individual was stealing small sums of money from my office in Iran," one man illustrated, "I wouldn't accuse him of it directly. Without mentioning the theft, I would talk to him, try to find out his problem, offer him help in that direction. If it was necessary to dismiss him, I would explain that the economic situation is so bad that he must find another position. In this way, I would avoid making an enemy, though he would know the reasons for my actions."

The importance of one's image extends to the outward appearance, and Iranians are quite conscious of the way people dress. The casual T-shirt, blue jeans, and tennis shoes attire of many American college students appears inappropriate to the newly arrived Iranian. Someone with a good position and education who does not dress accordingly is looked down upon and, as one man said, is considered a man too busy "counting money" or a miser.

"Every time you leave home in Tehran you have another way of behaving," said one Iranian professional woman. "You have to look perfect. In the United States there is a certain casualness — a look for work, for a date, for cocktail parties. When I return home I must quickly adjust to the more formal dress code."

One man associated the way people dress with *abru* by saying, "Attire can conceal reality. One may be poor, but the clothes conceal it." By contrast, in the United States it is the youth from wealthy families who often dress most poorly.

Sensitivity concerning one's family heritage is also a strong element in Iran. "I never hear an Iranian say his father was a poor man or a butcher," recounted one Iranian teacher. Once he remembered asking an American student what his father did for a living. The student replied, "He sells towels," and the embarrassed professor excused himself with a muffled "I'm sorry." "Why are you sorry?" asked the noncomprehending youth, and the even more confused professor exclaimed, "I'm sorry that I said I'm sorry!"

As a man born into a civilization thousands of years old, the Iranian also finds the American habit of identifying oneself by the nationality of one's forebears strange. The query of one American to another, "What nationality are you?" and a response such as "German, Scottish, and Irish" is seen by some Iranians as a sign that Americans are not really sure of themselves.

"Why do Americans say that they are Irish or Italian or English?" asked an international relations student. Another Iranian-born naturalized American citizen found it disconcerting when Americans asked him his nationality and rejected his answer of "American" by saying, "No, I mean where were you born?" Such a question, to an average American (virtually all of whom are descendants of immigrants within the last 200 years), would not have the significance it has to someone born into an ancient culture.

Contrasts between the American and Iranian family ties and relationships are many. The American parent sees his task as one of preparing his child to be completely self-reliant and independent of outside assistance as soon as possible. The Iranian parent, however, assists his child to fulfill his individual talents while at the same time stressing the necessity of smooth interpersonal relationships and especially the need for close family cooperation. Respect for authority, which conflicts with the American belief that each child or person should independently pursue autonomous goals, is emphasized in the Iranian family. Dependence upon others, in particular one's family, is not considered unnatural, as it would be in the American context.

A father visiting his 20-year-old son attending an American university commented, "Youth are taught to respect their parents in Iran. They refer to their parents in the formal tense all their lives. Without permission a boy would not speak before his father or even smoke a cigarette.

"A boy or girl is often under the sponsorship of the parents until he or she is 30 years old. A father would never say to his son, as he would in the United States, 'Now you are 18. You are independent and must support yourself in everything.' "

A girl student, commenting on the free and easy relationship between American children and their parents, said, "In the United States when the children are young, they share everything with the parents. In Iran the relationship is more distant and respectful, but it is longer lasting, and the children never lose touch with the parents."

Another young woman described family life in Iran as very close. "In the United States children are loved when small, but the parents appear tired of them by the time they are teenagers. You give them everything — car, college, etc. — but there is no time to love the child.

"In Iran the children would die for their parents. Parents are respected because of their love for us and because of their experience. We say they have 'worn a few more shirts than we have.' "

A young exchange student declared that he was startled by the answer of American students who, when asked why they are attending a university distant from their families, will invariably reply, "To get away from my parents, of course."

The American concept of setting up an independent existence as rapidly as possible appeared unfeeling to the Iranian, and he commented, "The kids don't give a damn about their parents."

"It's a sad situation," said one girl. "After the parents retire there is a great break for them. The children do not know what to do with them because the ties are not strong."

"Grandparents, even in the same city, do not get together often with their children and grandchildren," observed one student.

"In Iran we say that the young are 'the canes of our old age.' We know that we will be taken care of, just as we took care of them when they needed our help."

The American goal of maintaining an independent existence as long as possible, avoiding dependence upon anyone, even one's children, seems strange to the close-knit Iranians. An American family that lived in Tehran recounts that their Iranian friends were continually surprised when they learned that the head of the family's 79-year-old mother was living alone back in the United States and not with any other son or daughter. Although such a situation can at times be the result of neglect by the children, it is often the result of the pride of the American, however old, who wishes to be independent and sees dependence upon one's children as a failure at the end of one's life.

The idea of placing an aged or senile parent in a nursing home is appalling to the average Iranian, who sees it as the children's duty to take care of their parents. "If my mother is sick," said one, "we would take care of her at home." One person classified even the best nursing home as "a golden cage," and still another said with disapproval that only primitive tribes send their old and infirm off to die alone.

Differing concepts of life can sometimes have tragic consequences for people from different cultures if they lack the ability to understand the cultural differences of the other and to be flexible in their demands. A woman told of one instance where understanding, communication, and most important of all, the ability to compromise were lacking.

A couple, an Iranian husband and his American wife, were being divorced after years of marriage because the wife could no longer accept the fact that her husband felt totally responsible for his mother and unmarried sister. "I married you, not your family! You have to make a choice!" the American was supposed to have argued. The husband, on the other hand, had clear-cut responsibilities in Iranian society, and the marriage had reached an impasse.

"Who is right?" asked the young Iranian friend of the couple. She then answered her own question by exclaiming with a shake of her head, "They both are!"

11

EGYPT

An Egyptian living in the United States had a 6 p.m. appointment in his home with an American insurance agent. Ready to get down to business immediately, the agent was surprised when the Egyptian escorted him to the balcony and offered him a drink. He was even more startled when he was invited to dinner. As he got up from the dinner table, he turned to his host and said, "Surely you are not an American." The astonished agent had experienced his first taste of Egyptian hospitality. " 'Business is business' is the American way but not the Arab way. You have to socialize first in order to develop trust and faith, which are prerequisites to doing business," explained the Egyptian.

Whereas Egyptian hospitality can seem wildly extravagant by American standards, the more restrained American style of entertaining can seem downright ungenerous to the festive Arab. The two or three dishes served by the American hostess — carefully precounted to insure that the potatoes, vegetables, and meat slices are not wasted — would insult the guest in Egyptian society, where a 20-dish spread would involve two or three days of careful preparation.

"It is a bad reflection on the host to have nothing left over. Arabs have to make a feast, to have far more than what they will actually eat," according to one Egyptian.

Another aspect of Egyptian cordiality is the elaborate manner of greeting, beginning with *"El salam alako"* (Peace on you), continuing with several "Welcomes," and then moving to numerous inquiries about family and friends. This gradual easing into the topic at hand is true of formal seminars as well, and it proved somewhat irksome to an Egyptian who returned home for a series of meetings after adjusting to the more direct American style.

"I would try to push the topic forward; I felt I had a limited amount of time. Yet the first 15 minutes out of every hour were always devoted to an exchange of pleasantries," he said.

To the American, then, the Egyptian always seems to be wasting time. The Egyptian, on the other hand, feels that the American is a captive of the clock.

"Time for the Arabs has never been important. We're not always racing against time; we have all the time we need. It's a hard life but it's easygoing," said one Egyptian, who was himself somewhat disturbed by this snail's-pace approach.

Another Egyptian, however, after nearly three years in the U.S., looked back somewhat longingly on the "more relaxed, smooth" Egyptian style, epitomized by the expression "*Ma'a lesh,*" which translates roughly as "Take it easy," "Never mind," or "Don't worry."

"I was out of breath a whole year just trying to keep up with the industrialized system in the U.S. We are much more relaxed, we really are. In Egypt, people are generally home after 3 p.m.; you have the rest of the day to do what you want. In the U.S., I would leave home at 7 a.m. and come back after 6 p.m. — really exhausted. I couldn't even talk to my wife," he said.

The American's rigid adherence to a fixed time for lunch quickly caught his eye. "I would see a man work until 12 noon exactly and then stop — even if he was in the midst of drilling a hole. He would just put down the drill and go to eat," he added.

Yet another Egyptian felt that an overly relaxed attitude on the part of his fellow countrymen had led to stagnation — particularly in the all-encompassing government bureaucracy. "Government is *the* employer. Many civil servants feel their salary at the end of the month is almost their right for being born Egyptian; they are not expected to deliver anything. Thus you can see why a man doesn't do his job; he needs an incentive. The effect of this attitude is beginning to entrench itself, to take root. It's one of the serious problems facing Egypt."

How does a person combine the material well-being fostered by the discipline of the American puritan ethic with the emotional security afforded by the close-knit Egyptian family? The search for the missing link that would somehow blend these features of the two societies has bedeviled Egyptians living in the U.S., whose ambivalence was well expressed by a perceptive, philosophical Egyptian woman.

"I have to work constantly to keep the luxuries I enjoy in the U.S. It's like being hooked on alcohol. I don't know if I feel richer emotionally. I have lost a feeling of security; there is not the same kind of warmth and love as at home. Family ties are extremely, extremely important; they tie all of Egypt together. In the U.S., all of a sudden you are just an individual. I don't know whether it's worth it or not — all the hustle and bustle," she said.

"I like the luxuries but go through nightmares of whether I will be able to make it. If my husband dies, who would I go to? Nobody has time. It's like a tornado swallowing everybody in it. It's a vicious cycle: You have to make money to make payments to keep the luxuries; you have to neglect your own kin. The U.S. is a comfortable place to live but a lonely place to live. You gain conveniences but lose human security," she added.

What looks to the Egyptian like emotional security, however, can appear to the American to be an unwarranted intrusion on individual initiative. This difference in perspective was clearly illustrated in the comments of an Egyptian woman and an American woman, both of whom had raised children in the other's society.

"Our children have become Americanized. I'm not saying this is a bad culture, but it deprives them of personal richness. They're not getting anything here except a dollar now and then or a bicycle for their birthday; but they're not getting the experience of a total family — grandparents, uncles, and aunts. In Egypt, the child is an important person in many people's eyes, not just his mother's and father's," said the Egyptian woman.

Yet this omnipresent family concern in Egypt struck the American woman as a stultifying influence on the child's development.

"The children are dear little toys who are raised mainly by the mother. They are children for far too long and are given no responsibility in the home. There is communication between parents and children in the U.S. In Egypt the child is obedient and venerates his mother. The family ties are very strong, excessively strong in my opinion. It is the family that determines what the son's future will be and what the daughter will do," said the American woman.

The Egyptian is hit by the lack of warmth engendered by American individualism. The American is struck by the restrictive elements of the Egyptian extended family. Both views may be true, but clearly neither is the whole truth. For each embodies, perhaps inevitably, a built-in preference for one's own culture.

"Egypt is basically group oriented. The individual can't always do what he wants to do. He may have to do what the community wants him to do.

There is an intertwined relationship, particularly in the village. It's like a net," said one Egyptian, who explained that it was much easier for the individual to have his own way in the U.S. even if the community objects. "You try to raise children to be independent in the U.S. In Egypt they are always under the wing of the parents," added another man, who pointed out that a girl particularly would be protected until she was married and that until that time there would always be someone to guide her life.

Egyptian parents generally support their children through college, and along with responsibility for paying the bills goes a large measure of decision-making — selecting the university, the child's occupation, and ultimately the marriage partner. The cultural pattern of parental support tends to preclude even part-time work by the children.

When one Egyptian asked his cousin if she would not like to get a summer job, she declined, explaining that she would feel *aib* (shame), for it was beneath the dignity of the family. Others would think that her father didn't have enough money to support her.

Tight parental and religious control has led to traditional disapproval of boys and girls going out together or "dating," though the practice has found its way into the upper, educated circles of such urban centers as Cairo and Alexandria.

"But in the village, forget it. A boy would have to go out of the village if he wanted to go out with a girl," said one Egyptian.

"Normally girls don't smoke, drink, or hold hands with boys, though it is somewhat freer than when I was a girl," according to an Egyptian woman.

Yet there is still near-universal insistence on a virgin bride, and such American practices as mixed university dormitories and young people living together without being married are considered highly improper by the average Egyptian.

And even Egyptians who might accept dating as a general societal norm have some second thoughts when it hits to close to home.

"I might accept it — but not for my daughter. And I would beat up a guy who dated my sister just like he would probably beat me up if I dated his sister," one Egyptian said.

Though the vast majority of marriages are arranged by the parents, a young man can try to direct their attention to a girl who has caught his eye. But there is no such thing as "Hey, Mom and Dad, I want to get married," without any thought of the other family involved. For in Egypt both families work at preparing for the wedding day and view the marriage as more all-encompassing than the mere exchange of vows between individuals.

Nor is it an easy matter to marry across class lines. "We have different social classes, and these classes cannot merge. Even a rich, well-educated man from a lower class could not marry a poor, uneducated girl from a high social class. There would be too much shame," explained one man.

One enterprising Egyptian studying in the United States asked his family to line up some likely bridal prospects, then dashed back home to look them over.

"He interviewed 15 girls in 20 days, then narrowed his choice down to the three who most conformed to his ideal. But none of these families wanted their daughters to go to the U.S. Then he forgot about the whole thing and said he would get married in the States. But he had given Egyptian girls the first chance; his mind was at peace," explained an Egyptian man.

Coming from a family oriented society in which the elderly are revered for their wisdom, Egyptians are shocked by the treatment accorded old people in the youth-centered U.S. One woman spoke angrily of how American society neglects its senior citizens.

"The economic system and the puritan ethic have led to the idea that a person who is not constantly working is worthless. I resent that very strongly. I feel that a person who has given so much to society should be able to retire with respect and be considered a resource, a source of knowledge," said this woman, who has found her niche in American suburbia as a social worker with a senior citizens group.

Not only does she feel that she is making a contribution to American society, but she has also found in the faces of her elderly clientele images of her own grandparents and other relatives. She thus experiences a sense of Egyptian extended family and has been able in this way to make her own peace with American individualism.

Though a well-educated Egyptian woman can attain a preeminent place in society, at home she remains very much the traditional housewife and mother and in so doing readily accepts many of the traditional feminine stereotypes which are currently being challenged by American Women's Liberation activists.

"Egypt is a man's world; the wife takes a second place," said an

Egyptian woman matter-of-factly. "Yet she is powerful in the sense that she is respected by her husband and children. A man can have girl friends, smoke, and drink; nothing hurts his reputation. But a woman can't wear teeny-weeny miniskirts and sit around puffing cigarettes and drinking whiskey," she added, pointing out that most women are religious and accept this double standard.

"Femininity is a big thing. A well-educated, respected woman is very much behind her husband — supporting him, taking care of the children, acting in a demure, dignified manner, speaking in a low-pitched voice. Women's Lib in the U.S. is thus rejected to an extent because the woman is seen as losing her femininity," she said.

"A competent, professional woman — whose position may be as good as her husband's — still likes to have the man ahead of her. Her image is not shattered by his dominance. She likes to have him think he is the boss, though she may really be the boss," she added coyly.

At least one Egyptian man, however, was shocked to find that American women were not as liberated as he had been led to believe.

"We thought that American women were liberated, that they had it made. Yet the woman may be more of a slave in the U.S. — a slave to the machinery at home and with no outside help. The middle-class American woman is a mother and a cleaner and a cook, whereas her counterpart in Egypt usually does not have to cook and clean the house. If she does have to cook, there is someone to take care of the kids; and she won't have to drag out the vacuum cleaner," he said.

Another man tied the Egyptian male's predominant role to the Islamic ideal that the husband is the breadwinner and family protector and the wife is the child bearer and raiser. This traditional distinction has been blurred of late by increasing educational and employment opportunities for women.

"So there is Women's Lib in Egypt too. Women now have voting and job rights. But there is no open movement; rather it is gradual and indirect. Any change in Egypt must be gradual. If not, it is abnormal. Whereas with the accent on ambition and achievement in the U.S., more rapid changes can be accepted," he said.

Two aspects of Islam — the seeming ease of divorce and the right to have up to four wives — raise many an eyebrow in the non-Moslem world, but Egyptians insist that the actual text of the Koran is far stricter than is generally understood. Only by taking certain passages out of context has the belief arisen that a man can casually discard an unwanted mate and regally surround himself with a constantly changing stream of complaisant women.

For though divorce is allowed, the Koran specifies that it is the least acceptable thing which God permits one to do, that it is "the most hateful thing in the world," in the words of one Egyptian.

As for the four wives, once again this is allowed; but most people stop at this point and fail to note that the following passage in the Koran adds the stringent condition, "If a man can treat them justly and equally in all respects." Yet the Koran further states that man, being human, can never be just and equal to all.

"If you take the whole story together, it leads to the conclusion that one should not have more than one wife," commented an Egyptian, who pointed out that though an occasional villager will have more than one wife, the practice is by no means common.

Egyptians tend to see Islam as a more pervasive influence on their everyday lives than Christianity is on daily life in the U.S.

"Islam is very strict. The Koran states what is right and what is wrong in nearly every occasion that could arise in human life. It doesn't give you the chance to say, 'It's not in the book,' " explained one Egyptian.

Coming with a preconceived notion of general moral laxity in the U.S., some Egyptians are surprised to discover that a large segment of American society is more religious and conservative than they had imagined.

Egyptians arriving in the U.S. today are also often not prepared to cope with the competitive economic system and find their get-rich-quick dreams soon evaporating.

"Those who came to the U.S. 15 years ago were prepared to work long, hard years. Yet those arriving today figure that they can start out where the others are now. It takes them a long time to realize that the earlier arrivals had to struggle to make it," said one Egyptian.

The recent arrival is filled with conflicting impressions as he ventures out for his first look at American society. He is awed by the abundance of food at his fingertips, the spacious parks, and luxurious cars, but there is a lack of human contact in the streets that is sorely missed.

"The streets in Egypt are lively — filled with people going back and forth selling things. In the U.S. the streets are clean but so empty. It's like a ghost town. I wonder where all the people are," said a woman from Cairo.

"The U.S. is more organized. A line will form very quickly in the post office or department store, and there will be no cutting in line regardless of the person's position in society. In Egypt people know who is important and unimportant. So sometimes there are violations. A person will be given a place in line or a seat on the bus either because of his important position or out of sympathy for an older man or woman," added another Egyptian.

Though people working in service occupations in the two societies clearly occupy a low rung in the social order, the more hierarchical Egyptian pattern makes it more difficult for a service worker to escape his stigmatized status.

"In the U.S. a taxi driver or a janitor might drive a big Cadillac. If he is sitting next to you in the theater, you don't know what he does. In Egypt a taxi driver is a taxi driver — everywhere, all the time. I really don't like this, but it is a fact. The society is simply more structured in Egypt," commented an Egyptian who had lived for some time in the U.S.

"People are ashamed to do service jobs in Egypt. In the U.S., it doesn't matter; and there are few college graduates who have not been waiters or babysitters," he added.

Poles apart from the service personnel are the Egyptian university professors, who, in the words of one Egyptian, are "regarded as supreme masters. Their authority cannot be questioned." This high status accorded teachers is epitomized by the proverb, "Whoever teaches me a letter, I should become a slave to him forever."

"The situation is dramatically different in the U.S., where a person just happens to be a teacher. It's a job like any other, like an accountant, for example. There is no special relationship between teacher and students. It is thus very difficult for an Egyptian teacher when he first comes to the U.S. He might feel cheated, and his first reaction would be that the students are impolite," according to an Egyptian who has taught for some time in the U.S.

An Egyptian who had completed advanced studies in the States found American professors far more approachable than their Egyptian counterparts.

"A famous American professor, chairman, or chancellor doesn't show off his position. He might be on a first name basis with the janitor. In Egypt you talk to the professor in a certain way, to the department chairman in a more certain way, and to the rector not at all," he said.

Another Egyptian commented that American professionals such as doctors and lawyers tend to be more patient in dealing with their clients and more skilled in the art of listening than Egyptians in similar callings, who are often more hot-blooded and emotional.

Though it is at this point a rather tenuous theory, there may be a deeper reason for this seeming lack of patience on the part of the Egyptian professional. The American perhaps tends to think more inductively, that is, to reason from the particular to the general. Therefore he tends to need specific information or "feedback" from his client before he can make a decision. He must, in short, be a good listener. Such is not the case with the more deductive thinking Egyptian, who starts with the general theory and reasons down to the particular incident. He thus does not feel the same need for a smattering of details before coming to a conclusion. Rather he need only know the essence of his client's concern in order to plug in the appropriate answer based on his theoretical knowledge of the particular discipline.

Some support was given to this theory by an Egyptian whose wife is a medical doctor in the U.S. "She says that here in the U.S. you get the patient and listen to him; that's part of the game. Then comes the analysis (tests) to tell exactly what he has, but he is still suffering. In Egypt the doctor tries to find out more quickly what the patient has and may skip the analysis and rely on his own skill and his experience in handling similar cases," he said.

Whatever the validity concerning this theory of different patterns of thought, there can be no doubt that one of the major barriers to understanding between Egyptians and Americans is the expressive, emotional approach to life of the former and the reserved, pragmatic outlook of the latter. The most overt manifestation of this difference is, of course, the less inhibited Egyptian attitude toward physical contact — the way in which Egyptian men will hug and kiss one another and touch one another's hands and shoulders while talking.

An American anthropologist who lived in Egypt told how she had to get used to Egyptian closeness in situations where Americans would move apart or, anthropologically speaking, the use of "social space."

"In elevators Americans tend to stand far apart unless crowding forces them together, but in Egypt I could be the only one on the elevator and the other person would come over and stand right next to me. In a park, an American looks for an unoccupied bench or sits at the opposite end of a bench that is taken, but an Egyptian will sit right beside you," she said. Accompanying this preference for physical proximity is an emotional, animated approach to interpersonal relations, which makes the American suspicious. The Egyptian, on the other hand, mistrusts the American's measured, factual statements, for they seem to lack sincerity.

"Americans will say, 'Egyptians are too emotional; they are not logical or rational.' Egyptians will counter that you can't trust Americans because they don't have any feeling," explained the American anthropologist.

If a face to face encounter lacks emotional expressiveness, there seems little reason for the two people to get together to begin with; for as one Egyptian pointed out, "If you are only going to say, 'These are the facts,' you could write them and send them by mail.

"You feel that talking on the phone does not satisfy you as fully as getting together. In Egypt, the personal approach to conducting business is preferred to the telephone," he added.

"It helps in any argument to be able to quote from the Koran and literary works, but the importance of emotional expression is not limited to arguments. In ordinary street conversations a person might lose track of logic and continuity because of the emotion that is pouring out," according to another Egyptian.

While the American tends to listen for *what* is being said, the Egyptian will place greater emphasis on *who* is speaking and his relationship with the speaker.

"An Egyptian will ask, 'Do I like him? Can I trust him?' An American who starts spewing out statistics and facts may be rejected by the Egyptians because they do not like *him* rather than what he is saying," offered an American who has lived in Egypt.

Egyptians are aware of the difficulties their emotional approach can present for outsiders, who naturally must rely heavily on content since there is no way they can fathom the subtleties of the situation that are second nature to an Egyptian.

"It's a lot easier for us to adjust to the straightforward way than for others to adjust to our sinuous, complex way. An Egyptian will say, 'Judge me by what I do and not by what I say,' but this is hard for a Westerner to accept. When the Egyptian says, 'Don't take three-fourths of what I say,' the Westerner will say, 'Then why say it?' But it is a custom, a part of our culture. It may be partly because of the richness of the language. More elaborate words will sound better and be accepted more, whether or not they are more meaningful or true," said an Egyptian who had studied in the U.S.

Such an emotional underpinning causes Egyptians to be extremely sensitive to outsiders' comments, whether positive or negative. A small indication of good will arouses instant support. A slight insult causes it as quickly to disappear. As one Egyptian aptly expressed it, "A small word will get the whole country to your side, and a small word will lose it."

12

NIGERIA

The American's query, "What tribe are you from?" unsettled the Nigerian businessman, who immediately tried to ascertain by the inflection in the speaker's voice or the look on his face the real meaning behind the question. Was the remark merely a type of small talk coming from a basically well-meaning person whose knowledge of Africa and Nigeria was limited to "there are lots of tribes in Africa"? Or was it a question by someone who conceived of Africa as the "Dark Continent" inhabited by primitive nomadic groups of people? Or then again, was it a query of a person who knew Africa, appreciated its peoples and cultures, and was honestly interested in knowing more about the man with whom he was speaking?

The fact that three different perceptions of motivation for a simple phrase — frivolous, condescending, and serious — could flash through the Nigerian's mind is an apt demonstration that good intercultural relations are not simply a matter of good intentions and friendly conversation. A word, statement, or even a gesture can have different meanings for each of the parties involved.

"We resent being asked right off, 'What tribe are you from?' " declared one educator, who was asked his reaction to the common query. "Principally we resent it because we are Nigerians first and also because of the derogatory things that have been said about tribes in the past. After all, the colonial powers used the entire concept of the supposed 'primitiveness' of tribes and the alleged evils of tribalism to justify their foreign rule of Africa. When our students hear a non-African use such terms they are naturally, at first, suspicious of his or her motive."

Another Nigerian observed, "When someone asks me what tribe I am from, I usually respond by asking, 'What do you mean by tribe?' If he replies, 'I don't know,' I am really not very patient and often respond, 'If you don't know the meaning of the word, what good does it do to ask the question?'

"If, however, it's a sincere adult who is asking the question, I stop and explain the meaning of the word 'tribe' and how it can be applied in the Nigerian historical, cultural, and ethnic context.

"Africans do not have a word for that institution called a 'tribe.' Before the Europeans' arrival, we used the word 'country' for what now is labeled a 'tribe.' The word 'country' is currently used for the new nation-states artificially created by the European colonial administrators. If the Europeans had not intervened, Africa would obviously have developed new types of nation-states based upon their cultural groups, and many so-called 'tribes' would not be 'tribes' but countries. These days we prefer the words 'ethnic group' to 'tribe.' "

"It's all in the connotation of the word 'tribe,' " explained a Nigerian university professor. "How can you say that 11 million Yorubas or 11 million Hausas who belong to ancient and sophisticated cultures are members of a 'tribe'? Would you ask a Belgian if he were a member of the Flemish or French-speaking tribe? No, of course not!"

A Nigerian businessman said that his countrymen's sensitivity concerning the use of the word "tribe" had also increased as an aftermath of the recent civil war. "The word," he noted, "has acquired political connotations which we do not like to talk about now. Tribalism is one of the evils that plagued the First Republic and brought about the Civil War, so it is a detested thing. Today, we do not identify ourselves by tribe; we say instead that we are Nigerians from such and such a state."

The wide variety of emotions that can be stirred up by an unwary American's innocent question about ethnic origin can obviously jeopardize a new relationship. Used to identifying fellow countrymen by ethnic origin (Spanish-American, Italian-American, Irish-American) and usually not understanding the historical use of words such as "tribe" and "tribalism" as instruments of oppression for a multitude of African peoples, the American may be taken aback by the response to his inquiry. Such misunderstanding concerning the intentions of others can also occur in a wider range of areas.

The very sensitive field of respect for others and self-dignity is another prime example of an area where cultural customs often clash. A Nigerian noted in an address to an American student assembly that in some societies such as that of the U.S., expressions such as "Daddy, don't be silly," "Mommy, you're crazy," or "Uncle, that's a dumb thing to do" are not only commonly heard but are even regarded by some as indicative of the child's wisdom and maturity. In contrast, he declared, "I shudder to imagine what such impolite utterances would earn a Nigerian child who had the effrontery and temerity to utter them to his elders, much less to his parents."

"Respect for one's elders," he emphasized, "is sacrosanct and reflects discipline and good home training; disrespect is sacrilegious and portrays incorrigibility or lack of parental care."

The American child's seeming lack of courtesy toward his elders shocks and confuses the more formal Nigerians, who are even more profoundly disturbed when their own children begin to imitate their American playmates. "It's most strange — very disappointing," said one young agricultural economics student, in reference to the camaraderie that often exists between the American father and his son. "I saw a boy pat his father on the head and call him by his first name as a joke," he said, shaking his head in disbelief.

"We have such deep respect for each other; even my younger brother would not call me by my first name. I just could not raise children here!"

"When I first arrived for study," said a Nigerian professor, "I addressed everyone as 'Sir' and people laughed at me until I dropped it. Now I have children, and there is no respect. It is not 'yes, pa', it is simply 'yes.' I take it because I know where we are, but it is depressing."

Another young Nigerian father exclaimed with exasperation, "Children come home from school saying, 'Shut up!' or 'No'; why, to us it is repulsive! We never acted this way to our parents. We don't expect such behavior. Why, if they are not disciplined, they just look at you when you ask for something."

A student, commenting upon the different values under which American and Nigerian parents operate, said that in Nigeria "the young exist to help their parents while here the parents see themselves as existing to help the children." As children, he said, Nigerians are taught: "We raise you up to be a glory to your parents." His American classmates, he noted, however, stress their independence from their families and not their interdependence.

Accustomed to rules of respect which in some parts of Nigeria are expressed by the younger of two parties prostrating himself before an elder or averting his eyes as the elder speaks to him, the newly arrived Nigerian often finds adjustment to assertive American individualism jarring. A professional noted that he was at first startled when an

American child extended his hand in greeting without waiting for the African to take the initiative. The American parents beamed with approval at their son's good manners and adult behavior, he said, but he was surprised. In Nigeria such behavior would be considered bad manners, showing lack of respect for one's elders.

One man summed up the relationship between the old and young by declaring, "Whatever your station in society, however wealthy and successful you may be, you are expected to show respect for your elders." Another pointed out that while Nigerians will make temporary adjustments to American modes of behavior while in the United States, it is important to keep in mind that when in Nigeria one behaves differently. One of his friends, he said, forgot this maxim and upon returning to Nigeria with a doctorate declined to prostrate himself before his elders. "We say that such a man 'knows books, but he is not educated.' Even I," the 30-year-old man said, "avert my eyes when I am talking with my older brother."

The custom of averting or lowering one's eyes whenever an elder speaks caused problems for one Nigerian girl who arrived in the U.S. at age 14 to begin high school. "The teachers became angry," she recalled, "and demanded that I look them in their eyes when they addressed me."

The American parent's command to his child, "Look at me when I am speaking to you," bemused another Nigerian observer, who saw the American father becoming angry at what he conceived to be his offspring's sullen, disrespectful, or unseemly subservient behavior. "It is the opposite in my country," he exclaimed, "as eye to eye contact by a child would be universally construed as bold and disrespectful."

Manifestation of respect towards one's elders can also take other forms which in the American culture are susceptible to unfavorable interpretation. For instance, a government studies professor recounted how as a young student he once ran to help his American professor, who was carrying a heavily laden briefcase. He did this without thinking, for in Nigeria an older person would never be permitted by his juniors to carry a heavy object. The embarrassed American professor, however, held fast to his briefcase and told him simply, "We don't do that here, Michael."

Only later did the Nigerian realize that such a gesture would be seen by the American students as shameless flattery, placing both him and the teacher in an uncomfortable position. "Back home," he noted, "there would be no misunderstanding. It's simply a custom."

Another Nigerian tradition — giving token gifts to one's teachers — can also be the cause of misunderstanding. A Nigerian recounted how a friend who had been receiving a great deal of assistance from his thesis advisor decided to show his appreciation with a small gift. The American professor was shocked at the present and returned it, saying curtly that such a gesture was unnecessary. Never again, the Nigerian observed, was the relationship between the professor and student the same, much to the puzzlement of the student. One American student, however, scornfully said, "The African was trying to bribe the teacher."

His friend, the Nigerian said, was certainly not trying to curry favor, but was only expressing sincere appreciation in a way that would be perfectly acceptable in his own cultural environment.

The same man recalled how he, as a student, had once dashed over to a professor to hold an umbrella for him as he crossed in the rain between two buildings. His egalitarian-minded American fellow students were shocked at this gesture and asked incredulously, "Why did you do that?" Now, he said with a shrug and a smile, he behaves just as the Americans do.

The Nigerian belief that the welfare of children is a community concern in which all adults have a responsibility is another concept that clashes with American ideals of small nuclear families and noninterference in others' affairs.

"Back home if you see a boy on the street misbehaving, you stop and admonish him whether he is any relation to you or not. Here if you tell a child, 'That is wrong,' he will retort, 'You're not my father; mind your own business.' " I saw a boy throwing rocks at a building and went to tell his mother. Instead of expressing appreciation, she told me, "I didn't employ you as a babysitter for my child!"

Another Nigerian told of a similar incident in which he went to the apartment of the father of a youngster who with others was stoning a property guard in an effort to drive him off so they could steal some building material. "I expected the father to thank me and rush out to stop the affair. However, instead of listening to me, the boy's father declared angrily, 'That's my son; mind your own business! Leave him alone!'

"A little while later the police came, arrested the boys, and the parents were called to the station to retrieve their children. The father came to me later and apologized, saying he acted on impulse. 'I'm sorry I spoke to you the way I did; I was wrong,' he said, but his first idea, that I had no business in the matter, made me feel very bad."

The readiness to intervene to right a wrong or to stop something that should not happen is, according to the Nigerians, something very characteristic of all the country's ethnic groups. "If a man cries out for help, all the neighbors' doors fly open. Something illegal such as thievery is considered a public affair in Nigeria. Action is not considered meddling in the affairs of others. People protect their neighbors' goods as if they were their own property and defend the owners' rights if they are absent."

A Nigerian said that he thought that this feeling of communal responsibility could be credited as an important factor in stopping violent deeds before they become major incidents. "For example, if I were beating my wife and she were screaming, a neighbor would feel it his duty to intervene. He could come right into my home, ask what the problem was, and if necessary give my wife temporary shelter with his family. Then he would come back and talk with me and try to resolve the problem. I would not be angry with him for interfering; I would be grateful for his concern," he said with emphasis.

Noting that the traditional Nigerian marriage is essentially a contractual agreement between two families, not between two individuals, one Nigerian declared that in time of domestic estrangement the families of each side would meet to adjudicate the couple's differences. "Again, because of our respect for elders, the settlement is accepted by the couple, and there ends their disagreement."

In the United States, noted a Nigerian educator, "a girl often gets married without her parents even knowing their son-in-law. Here, just as it is easy to marry, it is also easy to break a marriage. That brings tragedy not only to the husband and wife but also to their children and their relatives.

"When I was a student, I wrote my mother that I was going to look for a wife in America. She wrote back, 'Remember, I must know who you are going to marry, know her parents, see her character.' " The impossibility of achieving this caused him to leave school in order to work and earn passage money for a return to Nigeria. Once home, he recounted, his parents set to work negotiating with the parents of eligible girls for a future bride. After the parents of each had checked the other's character, and he had agreed to his parents' choice, the marriage was performed. Although he could have rejected his parents' judgment, such a course of action would have been rare. One man described the question of consent on the part of the couple as virtually automatic "because our culture is such that a child has faith in his parents and has confidence in their ability to make prudent decisions and safeguard his interest and welfare."

"Americans misunderstand the idea of dowry," said one. "It isn't true that we 'buy' our wives. The parents of the groom make a gift to the parents of the girl on the day of the marriage, but the bride's parents return this gift in other goods given to the daughter to set up housekeeping in her new home — clothes, cooking utensils, glassware, etc."

"There is nothing strange in our traditional marriage system," affirmed a Nigerian. "The history of Europe is replete with examples of arranged monarchial marriages by which the prince of one kingdom and the princess of another kingdom were joined together in holy wedlock without their consent. Our first parents, Adam and Eve, were offered to each other by God; their marriage was not a product of the principle of consent.

"Americans say that their marriages are between equal partners, but that promotes instability. We say a ship cannot have two captains or the ship will sink." An educator observed, "In Nigeria it is the man who is the indisputable captain."

"Back home," said another, "a woman knows she is not the equal of her husband. He is the head of the house and has the last say in everything. For instance, a woman knows it is her duty to carry packages unless they are too heavy and then her husband will help.

"Here men accompany their wives to the supermarket and carry everything. It seems ridiculous for us to see a man pushing a shopping cart. The market is the place for women."

Another man commented, "Marriages in Nigeria are mostly to have children. A childless marriage is a great concern to all the family. Men must have issue before dying. As a child-conscious people, we cannot understand those women who say, 'I don't want to have any children.' Nigerian women love children."

One Nigerian pointed out an additional contrast in marriage views by saying that if a Nigerian husband and wife had differences that could not be resolved through family mediation, it would be the wife who would be forced out of the home, not the husband. "It's inconceivable to us," he said strongly, "that a wife could have the police eject the husband."

In the rare case of a marriage breakup it is the father who has custody of the children, and it is he who keeps the home, quite the opposite of the usual American practice. "Who is more fitted to have control of the home and children than the man?" asked one student rhetorically. Another pointed out that if the woman remarried, the children of her first husband would never be recognized as his own by her second husband.

"The Nigerian extended family system presents a very difficult hurdle for a foreign wife," a professor acknowledged. "An English woman told me, 'It's slavish because you have to respect so many people.' When a Nigerian man marries a non-African, he is under pressure from his wife to change. People then look down on you as a 'henpecked man'; they think you are weak. A wife is expected to take part in family life."

Many financially strapped Nigerian students expressed some discomfort with requests from relatives in their homeland. One complained, "They expect so much from us as if we could pick up money on the streets; it's a major problem."

Another noted, "Relatives write to say they need this or that without thinking how we can get it; in Africa they believe that this is a rich country and that dollars are plentiful." None, however, objected to the principle that better-off relatives are dutybound to assist the less fortunate members of an extended family, which includes all living relatives.

Describing the sense of security the much broader Nigerian concept of family gives its members, an offical said it is a good substitute for the educational endowments and life insurance plans of other countries.

"Old age does not pose a serious threat. The fact that your parents are poor or are dead does not seal your aspiration for further education; that you are jobless through no fault of yours does not mean that you will starve. If as a result of having lost your job you can no longer pay your house rent, take it easy; you and your wife and children will be sheltered by one of your relatives, and all of you will be fed and fully taken care of."

Nigerians report that even English, a common official language for both their own nation and the United States, can sometimes be an impediment to better intercultural communication. Stressing that one should be prepared for many semantic differences as well as a variety of regional accents, one professor remarked that during his student days in the United States he would be continuously irritated if someone would bump him and say "Excuse me" instead of "I'm sorry." The phrase "Excuse me" — a correct form of apology in American English — has, he noted, an entirely different meaning in Nigeria. "It means 'Get out of my way; let me pass.'"

Colloquial phrases that many Americans use impolitely but usually without malice, such as "You're crazy," or "You're stupid," or "Oh, shut up!" can, when said to a Nigerian, cause severe misunderstanding.

"While working at my factory job I was having a political argument with a fellow worker," recalled one Nigerian. "The woman next to me interrupted to say, 'Oh, shut up! You don't know what you're talking about.' I was shocked and asked her to repeat herself, which she did. It was difficult to control my fury, and I said, 'You, a *woman*, are telling me, a *man*, to shut up! ' Then I pushed her. She began to cry, and a crowd gathered. No one would listen to my explanation, and they all said I would be dismissed.

"When the foreman came over, they said that I had pushed the woman for no reason at all. He asked me if that was true and I said, 'Of course not; the woman has insulted me, telling me to shut up without provocation.' He seemed stunned at this explanation and left, saying he had to think the matter over.

"Later the foreman called us both to his office. After questioning me about what I found offensive in the remark, he advised restraint in the future. The woman was also warned to be cautious with me, that I came from a different culture, and that she should think before using slang."

Another Nigerian told of how he had ordered an unfortunate American passenger out of his cab when she, having lost an argument about the best route to a certain location, declared in exasperation, "Oh, you're crazy!" The furious passenger, upon leaving the cab, immediately flagged down a passing police patrol car to register a complaint. "The police officer," the Nigerian remembered with a smile, "must have had previous experience with foreigners. He took the time to explain that I should not take offense at such comments."

A more serious misunderstanding involving difficulty with regional accents was cited by one Nigerian as the cause of bad feelings between black Americans and some Nigerians. He told of how four of his countrymen had, soon after their arrival in the United States, gone to a restaurant for dinner. A black waitress asked if she could take their orders, but because of her southern accent the Nigerians could not understand her. After some confusion they said they really did not want anything and left the restaurant.

The incident upset the Nigerians, as they worried that the waitress would consider their departure a "racial" slight; and they decided to return to the dining room. In the intervening 15 minutes, however, the black waitress had gone on her lunch break and been replaced by a co-worker who was white. The Nigerians had no trouble understanding the second waitress's northern-accented English and reluctantly ordered their meals from her. To their chagrin, however, the black waitress saw them ordering from her white substitute and was visibly furious at what indeed did appear to be discrimination.

Relations between black or Afro-Americans and Nigerians can suffer from such misunderstandings. As black foreigners in a country in the midst of what some political scientists have categorized "a social revolution" aimed at eradicating racism, Nigerians often find themselves in a difficult position. "Many Afro-Americans think we should participate in the Black Power and civil rights movements," said one Nigerian student leader, "but we cannot because this is not our country. If we have white friends," he said with distress, "we are scorned by some more militant Afro-Americans. It's difficult to fit in."

Another student, who cited an incident in which he encountered illegal discrimination in housing, said, "Still, since you are a foreigner, you cannot really criticize. Maybe the difference, the reason for the strain, where it exists, is that we Nigerians know we have a home to return to; all this is a temporary thing to us. The Afro-Americans, however, have no alternative; they have to struggle against such practices."

Still other Nigerians, however, minimize such differences between black or white Americans and Africans. An American student of African studies said, "The key to good human relations among the different races and nationalities is, I think, to break down the stereotypes that the African has of the American and that the American has of the African." A Nigerian agreed, concluding, "One should not try to transplant ideas from home. Each society is different, and we can learn a great deal from one another by observing the different ways we respond to common problems."

PERSPECTIVES

Most of the comparisons in the foregoing chapters were made by international visitors who had lived some time in the United States and had consequently had the opportunity to reflect on cultural differences based on their own experiences. But what of the recent arrival, the type of person we at the International Center are trying to assist in making an immediate adjustment to life in the U.S.? What are his concerns as he ventures out into American society?

We have had an excellent vantage point from which to make some observations along these lines, for during the past four years we have been concluding our weekly program with a session entitled "Reflections on the Week's Experience." Visitors have been urged to comment on their experiences outside the Center in light of cultural differences. What aspects of their daily interaction with Americans have been most difficult to understand, accept, and adjust to?

If a single word could summarize the unpredictable and often highly perceptive comments of the visitors it would be "ambivalence." They are generally impressed by the efficiency, organization, and orderliness of American society but are disturbed by what they view as an overly blunt, brusque approach to interpersonal relations.

A Nepalese visitor, for example, found it "difficult to adjust to the mechanized way of life in the U.S. Everybody is busy; there are pushbuttons for everything. This society is individualistic. Sometimes people help, but often they are busy in their own rut." Yet a Brazilian commented favorably on American frankness and ability to organize. "Everything is so well planned," he said.

The idea, of course, is neither to bury nor to praise American society but rather to begin to understand it and in so doing to better understand one's own culture and values. For if a visitor can comprehend intellectually and discuss analytically why Americans act the way they do, he should be better able to adjust emotionally to the unfamiliar practices he encounters here.

Initially many visitors are upset by the way Americans tend to sit by themselves in buses and cafeterias and walk briskly by with a hurried "Hi" rather than stopping to chat in the street, as would be the custom in their homelands. But railing against such practices is not going to change them, and a visitor's sojourn will certainly be more pleasant and productive if he can see the reason for the different behavioral pattern and accept it as a cultural difference instead of wasting emotional energy through repeated displays of unremitting hostility. In fact, experiences which would otherwise be unpleasant can be a source of expanded awareness, if a person is only able to detach himself sufficiently from the emotional aspect of the situation so as to view it as an educational opportunity.

Before discussing the specific areas which are of most concern to the new arrival, mention should be made of some of the hidden difficulties encountered in trying to discuss cultural differences with groups so heterogeneous in terms of customs, English language ability, and exposure to other cultures. These beneath-the-surface problems, which can be broken down into four categories, must be taken into account by anyone who plans to conduct an intercultural seminar. For without an understanding of some of the underlying motives and attitudes which can color a participant's involvement, the discussion leader will be needlessly disheartened by a lack of response or be unable to untangle a genuine cultural difference from the subjective interpretation of it by the speaker.

PARTICIPATION

The first roadblock to a successful discussion has undoubtedly been encountered by anyone who has ever had much contact with Asians, particularly Southeast Asians. The problem essentially is this: how do you involve persons in an analytical public discussion when everything in their cultural heritage has tended to inhibit — rather than encourage — participation in such an open, forthright forum. To quote a Vietnamese saying, "When the mouth works, the mind and hands don't work."

Such an expression does not square very well with the Western notion of a Socratic dialogue. A rational, analytical approach — at least in public — is obviously a discomforting one to the average Southeast Asian, who puts the heart over the head, intuition over reason, and silence over unnecessary speech. The message of the American speaker may be coming through loud — if not always clear — to the Southeast Asian, but one outside his culture would never know it; and thus the American strives valiantly, but vainly, to elicit the feedback which is the key to his success as a communicator.

Take the case of the Thai woman and the American woman at lunch. The American woman kept trying to draw the Thai out with questions about home, family, job, interests, hobbies — but nothing worked. Afterwards the American woman, totally frustrated (a word which does not translate adequately into Thai), complained about her lack of response. The Thai woman, for her part, could not understand why she had been subjected to the third degree by her incessant inquisitor.

After one "Reflections" session, a Thai approached apologetically to explain the lack of participation by his country's contingent. He pointed out that even for someone like him — who had been in the U.S. before and spoke good English — it was difficult to speak out in public. Thus it was twice as hard for the newly arrived.

Interestingly enough, we have found that a single Southeast Asian will often more readily participate than he would if fellow countrymen were present. No longer need he concern himself with the possible opprobrium such conduct might bring about in the presence of his cultural peers.

The important thing to remember is that lack of participation should not be equated with lack of interest. Often a Southeast Asian will follow the discussion closely but wait until the formal session is over to bring up some salient point privately.

Naturally it is impossible for the Southeast Asian to immediately shunt aside years of cultural conditioning and readily accustom himself to the participatory American pattern. At the same time, however, he should be made aware of the different expectations of the American government official, business executive, or university professor with whom he will be training or studying. Hopefully, he will gradually feel more comfortable with the direct American style and learn to live with it while in the U.S. An Indonesian, in giving his country's version of "When in Rome...," neatly summed up the need to adjust when he said simply, "Different fish, different pond."

FOREST FOR THE TREES

A second hindrance to the accurate analysis of cultural differences might be termed the "forest for the trees" dilemma. A person who has spent his entire life within the familiar cultural context of his homeland will tend to magnify the differences within his own society and thus be unable to pick out underlying patterns of culture which differentiate his civilization from others. Unable to generalize about his own culture, he is even less able to discern the underlying patterns of behavior in the new society, for he simply lacks the experience which would enable him to cut through the *intra*cultural differences of the two societies and see more clearly the *inter*cultural variances.

Perhaps the most that can be done for someone in this situation is to simply introduce him to the idea of intercultural differences by setting out some of the underlying values and attitudes in his and American society and by illustrating them through concrete examples. For example, one can point out that Americans tend to be more self-reliant and that members of his society tend to be more interdependent and to exemplify the difference by indicating that young people in the U.S. want to set up their own households, whereas in his society it would be heartless to send the young out on their own. Or, explain that in the U.S. individuals choose their own marriage partner, whereas in his society marriage is much more a merger of two families.

We have found it helpful in this regard to pass out a chart which compares the underlying values and attitudes in American society with those of a directly contrasting culture. The visitor is urged to analyze the cultural patterns of his own society in relation to the two societies given. Though the differences may not be perceived clearly at first, they should come into sharper focus as he becomes more familiar with American society. At least he has been given a tool and a technique to assist in his gradual awareness of cultural differences.

I AM MY CULTURE

The next barrier to a more profound insight into cultural differences could be termed the "I-am-my-culture" problem. An individual may mistakenly equate a personal characteristic with a general cultural trait and thereby fail to realize that the overall thrust in his own society is toward a pattern which he *personally* does not happen to embody. An outspoken Southeast Asian might conclude that his people are direct and blunt, or a somber Brazilian might maintain that his society is generally serious and reserved. Similarly, an American environmentalist who personally feels that man must harmonize with his surroundings might challenge the idea that Americans have historically viewed nature as a force outside man that must be regulated and controlled. Yet a moment's reflection indicates that there would be no need for the environmental movement at all if the majority of Americans had traditionally treated nature as he did.

When someone makes what you view to be a mistaken assumption about his society based on your previous experiences, the natural reaction is to rush to judgment, to cite a series of instances which will disprove his contention, and rest assured that he has been made to see the error of his ways. This approach obviously contributes little to improved intercultural understanding, for the individual in question only feels that you do not understand his society and is embittered by the way you challenged him before the group. Far better is the technique of asking others from his own culture to comment on his observations, for often they will be able to point out general cultural characteristics of which he was unaware but which he will accept as valid when pointed out by a majority of his own countrymen. Thus he is forced to take a fresh look at his own personality in relation to the general cultural norm and may finally agree that his own conduct or attitude — at least in this instance — does not conform to the typical pattern in his society.

LIKE IT ISN'T

What about the visitor who simply will not accept the notion that cultures are different, who says that he has found everything in the U.S. exactly as he was accustomed to at home? He foresees no adjustment problems, for there is nothing different to adjust to; he describes his society as a mirror image of American institutions, and he seems generally to be telling it "like it isn't." Is such an individual out to deceive, is he totally imperceptive, or is he aware of some deep universal truth that has eluded his fellow countrymen and the anthropologists who have studied his society?

This reaction can perhaps be explained in two ways. Many of the participants in our program are from urban centers, and there is some truth to the contention that a certain commonality exists among city dwellers worldwide — whether it be in New York, Paris, Tokyo, Bangkok, Lagos, Delhi, or Rio. In *any* urban area life tends to be more impersonal, clock-conscious, and cosmopolitan and less leisurely, group-centered, and less traditional than in that country's rural sector. Thus an urbanite may feel at least superficially more at home in a foreign metropolis than he would in the hinterlands of his own country. He has lost touch — if indeed he ever had any contact — with the traditions, attitudes, and values which shape the daily lives of the majority of his fellow countrymen.

Thus one reason that a visitor cannot make intercultural comparisons is that he is genuinely ignorant of his own historical values because he has grown up in an environment which is far removed — physically, intellectually, and emotionally — from the traditionally dominant pattern. But a second, more subtle, influence is often at work as well, for a visitor may be thoroughly familiar with the underlying patterns of culture in his society but be reluctant to discuss them, feeling that they are somehow backward or out of step with what he has come to accept as the more "modern" American (or Western) cultural pattern. It is not easy for one outside his culture to know whether to attribute this seeming imperception to ignorance or reticence. It may well be a combination of the two.

A Jordanian once sharply challenged the notion that customs in his society differed from those in the United States, pointing out that punctuality was important, that the welcome was not a slow, gradual process, and that one did not initially refuse more food when it was offered by the hostess. This seemed to run counter to what others from his culture had said previously, but it is not easy to dispute such a strongly held position. It was only in the social hour after the "Reflections" session itself that an Indian pursued the matter further. "You have adapted to the Western style like I have, but this is surely not your traditional way," he said, adding that he himself had to distinguish between the way he acted when he was with Westerners and the more traditional Indian style.

Having looked at some of the hidden hindrances to a satisfactory intercultural dialogue, we are now ready to discuss the specific areas that are of most concern to the recent arrival in the U.S. Though observations in the "Reflections" session can range from food ("Even the Cokes are sweeter here.") to football ("Why did the priest at Mass say a prayer for the 'Redskins'?"), comments concerning 12 aspects of American life stand out conspicuously as we look back over the past four years. Since we purposely allow as much leeway as possible for visitors to bring up issues that are of interest to them, we feel that the 12-part pattern which has emerged could serve as a guide for others involved in intercultural orientation. The 12 topics that follow — whether directly or indirectly, whether in a positive or negative tone — surface in our sessions with a striking regularity.

1. PACE OF LIFE

Visitors from a variety of African, Asian, and Latin American countries clearly agree on one thing: the American is a man on the go, racing the clock from dawn to dusk, obviously in pursuit of something which seems just beyond his grasp. What makes him run? Where is he going? And why must he hurry so? A smattering of comments from several cultural perspectives indicates the amazement with which the new arrival regards the pace of life in the U.S.

"Americans are task-oriented, businesslike. They always walk briskly, purposefully, as if there were a task to do. It is different in the Philippines; one will slowly greet another and often invite him for coffee," commented one visitor.

A fellow countryman found American people "tense and jittery but always smiling and trying to be friendly." The fact that a high school would begin a class at 10:47 was incomprehensible to a girl from Colombia. "It's like *hora de avion* (airline time)," she said. A Vietnamese visitor was similarly startled to find that a liquor dealer would not sell alcohol just three minutes before such a sale was forbidden by a Sunday blue law. "Americans have no time to rest," added another Vietnamese. "Even in the cafeteria, a person eats, then just dashes out."

Particularly disheartening to many visitors is the way Americans tend to "ignore" them in the cafeteria and on the bus, and offer, from the perspective of their cultures, too few words of welcome. A Ghanaian pointed out that there would be more of an exchange of pleasantries on meeting someone in the street in his country. "I don't like to say just 'Hi,' but I think I'm getting used to it," he said.

A Tanzanian felt keenly the "lonely crowd" aspect of life in a large American city. "I am just a foreigner, and nobody cares where I come from. They just push around and go their own ways." Though he understood that this was part of the "do-it-yourself, be-on-your-own" style of life in the U.S., it still bothered him because it was so different from the more leisurely pace he was accustomed to at home.

New York, the epitome of the fast-paced life style, is not a favorite first stop for many visitors. "In New York I felt crushed, like under a skyscraper," said a woman from Viet Nam. "I had to go every day to the World Trade Center. I always had to rush from morning until evening. We walk very slowly in my country, but here if you don't rush, you will be caught up in a turnstyle or a revolving door; you have to be ready to jump out. In Viet Nam we work from 8 a.m. to noon, then take a nap until 2:30 and work again until 6 p.m. There is time to have fun," she added. But pace is relative, as a Saudi Arabian was quick to point out. "If you think Americans are fast, you should go to Germany and see how they walk."

2. FRIENDSHIP

Industrialization and urbanization have led to a highly mobile American society, in which the average person moves 14 times in his lifetime. When this mobility factor is combined with the individualistic bent which has long been part of the American national character, the result is a concept of friendship that seems to lack the depth and permanence which such a relationship demands in a more traditional society.

Though many visitors find Americans friendly enough, they find it difficult to establish the same type of all-embracing reciprocal relationship that they are accustomed to at home. The easy approachability of Americans is misleading in that it conjures up expectations of a deep friendship which is often not forthcoming. This is because in many societies there is much more initial reserve in interpersonal relations, particularly with strangers. Once a relationship approaches the point of gregariousness that Americans take as a normal starting point, it would indicate that the barriers between the two individuals had broken down and that the prospect of a close relationship was in the offing. For many visitors, the American comes on too strong too soon and then fails to follow-up with the implicitly promised friendship. The American, for his part, can be annoyed by the demands placed on his time and energies by "someone he scarcely knows."

It was failure to understand the gradual, deliberate approach to friendship in his society that made it difficult for Americans to comprehend the Vietnamese mentality, according to one visitor. "One must enter the Vietnamese personality little by little — like an osmosis," he said.

Some visitors see the "American" friendship pattern as characteristic of the urban, industrialized areas of their homelands as well and thus draw a distinction between the more easily uprooted friendships necessitated by city life and the chance for deeper, long-lasting relationships which the traditional, permanent rural setting provides.

Evidence of the American's "insincerity" is sometimes found in the custom of the "Dutch treat." The visitor understands that he has been invited out to lunch or dinner, only to find himself the recipient of a separate check. We must repeatedly explain that from the American viewpoint this custom is not ungenerous or stingy and then alert the visitor to the subtle but important distinction between "Let's go to dinner" and "I'd like to *take* you to dinner."

One extremely important point to impress on the newly arrived visitor is the need to take the initiative in his dealings with Americans. As an Indonesian student explained, "The first week American students were so cool. No one approached me to ask some friendly questions as we always do in our country when a foreign student arrives. This also happened in social gatherings among Americans. It took me about a month to understand that the host country people were not going to take the initiative in such gatherings. After that, I just jumped in without waiting until someone else approached me."

"The better you explain yourself, the better you will be understood," was the advice of a visitor from Sierra Leone.

The way in which an American can compartmentalize his emotional life has been a source of wonderment to several visitors, including a Nepalese woman who roomed with several American students. "All week long they would concentrate intensely on their studies; then on Friday night they seemed to change personalities. Studies were forgotten for the joys of the weekend. Yet on Sunday, they would switch back to normal. It was a most marvelous thing," she said.

Following a Saturday night date with an American coed, a Vietnamese was startled the following Monday when she brushed by him in the hall with barely a sign of recognition. "It was almost as if she didn't know me. I later learned that Americans make a sharp distinction between time for study and time for social life. We don't organize our lives in that way," he said.

An Indian added a slightly different wrinkle when he said that an American in his country would encounter the opposite problem. A girl might be very friendly to him during the day but ignore him completely if he tried to ask her out at night. Like many other visitors, he felt that the intrusion of dating into his society — whether considered right or wrong — was a change that could not be stopped.

3. SERVICE AND EGALITARIANISM

One of the most sensitive yet essential issues is the whole question of attitudes towards and expectations of people in the service occupations — taxi driver, waitress, bellboy, store clerk, etc. The other side of the coin must be considered too, that is, the attitude of these people towards the international visitor. We, in a sense, are caught in a crossfire between the two groups. To hear some visitors tell it, polite service people are as rare as a cab on a rainy day in Washington. When we give equal time to hotel and restaurant managers, they sometimes fashion a stereotype of the arrogant, abusive foreign visitor. The truth is not somewhere in between. Rather, it seems, both sides are right — if one considers their respective cultural vantage points. This doesn't make it any easier for either group to understand, let alone accept. The root of the problem seems to be this: high-ranking members of hierarchical societies are suddenly confronted with the tough, leveling effect of American egalitarianism.

It is not easy for an elite member of a hierarchy to see many benefits in a more egalitarian order. Accustomed to instantaneous, cordial (and from the American point of view, fawning) service at home, he suddenly has this base of service support pulled out from under him, and he is left to make do in the kitchen, grocery store, and laundromat — foreign territory for many a male visitor. To add insult to injury, he must confront surly service in the drug store, restaurant, and hotel.

Often visitors will complain that store clerks do not seem "interested" in waiting on them. An Ethiopian, for example, claimed that waiters "didn't have any initiative." According to a Nigerian, "The salesmen are not cheerful. They have no ambition to show you anything or ask questions." An Indonesian found taxi drivers and waiters "rude and impatient."

If one is expecting discriminatory treatment, it is easy to read prejudice into any supposed slight: a taxi driver who zooms by, a waiter who does not rush to serve, a store clerk who does not offer a kind word. "It must be that they are discriminating against me because I am a foreigner" is a natural thought, until the visitor is made aware that Americans suffer the same treatment.

A Jamaican, for instance, found bus drivers totally nondiscriminatory with their unfriendly phrases. "They're pretty crude," he said. "If I ask them for directions, they ask me, 'Can't you read?' And it's not just because I'm a foreigner; I hear them snapping at their own nationals."

But participants in our program are also urged to consider how some of their customs can rub American service people the wrong way. In many societies, for example, one would call a waiter by slapping the table, snapping his fingers, or letting out a loud whistle — conduct that is not geared to win the hearts and minds of American restaurant workers. A Kenyan told how a clerk ordered him out of a store after he had whistled shrilly to show his amazement and disappointment when told the price of an article.

The real difficulty lies in trying to explain why an American service person with his "I'm-as-good-as-the-next-guy" attitude is easily antagonized when he receives what he perceives as an order from his customer, when he feels that he is being treated as an inferior. This explanation is often incomprehensible to someone raised in a society where both the customer and the service person believe that it is the duty of the latter to perform with interest and politeness.

"The idea that should exist in the U.S. doesn't exist. The service people should feel that it is their duty to perform these services," concluded an Ethiopian simply. A Pakistani placed an even greater burden on the service person by insisting that he had a double duty to render proper treatment: his offical duty and his "moral" duty.

Some visitors come to sense that the more egalitarian American pattern tends to preclude any feeling on the part of the service person that he is "dutybound," for this to him connotes a master/servant, superior/inferior relationship which instinctively repels him. A Vietnamese quickly noted this egalitarianism in an American restaurant. "At first I thought the waitress belonged to the lower class, but she treated me just like any other customer — no more, no less — and screamed out, 'hard boiled eggs.' She didn't act humble like a street vendor in my country." Though he had come prepared to treat service people as equals, a Chinese visitor was still somewhat taken aback when he found that they also treated *him* like an equal.

A perceptive Kenyan noted an inherent contradiction in the American and Kenyan attitudes towards service. Americans, because they do not feel subservient, do not take pride in doing a job they consider menial. Yet this seems to conflict with another American idea that any type of labor is ennobling. Kenyan service people, who undoubtedly do feel a measure of subservience, feel more comfortable in performing a service job and take pride in doing it well — and this in a society that does not consider manual labor ennobling.

The pinch of egalitarianism, coupled with a greatly reduced living standard relative to the society, can lead to the phenomenon known as "role-shock" for a visitor with a prominent position back home who must suddenly conform to his new-found role as a mere university student. As one Tanzanian sadly summarized the situation, "We have a certain status in life, and here we make less than a dishwasher." And the very fact that his plight will fail to evoke a sympathetic response from the average egalitarian-minded American will make his adjustment just that much more difficult. He — like many a high-ranking visitor — has suddenly become, to borrow the Indonesian maxim, a different fish in a decidedly different pond. He will stay afloat only if he can somehow effect, if not a permanent peace, at least a temporary truce with American egalitarianism.

4. EMOTIONAL EXPRESSIVENESS

From Mexico to Argentina, Ecuador to Brazil, our neighbors to the south are convinced that Americans are, in the words of one Nicaraguan, *"hombres de hielo"* (men of ice). By their standards, we stand far apart when we talk, greet without any feeling, and generally display a cold, distant demeanor as we race about our daily chores. "No one holds hands, not even the children," observed one Brazilian.

Yet to visitors from Asia, this American "man of ice" can seem a burning tinder box of flashing emotions. Thais, for example, sometimes use the words *jai rawn* (hot-hearted) to describe what they view as impulsive, choleric conduct by the American. This hot-hearted man of ice clearly stands near the center of an emotional spectrum which extends out to embrace the effervescent Latins at one extreme and the cooly subdued Southeast Asians at the other.

Whereas Latins are troubled by what they view as our understated adjectives, Asians wonder why we have to exaggerate so. In Spanish, one cannot say that a movie is merely "good" or even "very good." It must be "magnificent," "stupendous," or "fantastic" before anyone would waste time going to see it. An Indian, on the other hand, felt that Americans loved hyperbole, that something always had to be "great" or "spectacular."

Southeast Asians sometimes mention Americans' penchant for praise — whether it be of food, dress, or household furnishings — and the frequency of the effusive "thank you" following a complimentary comment. An Ethiopian pointed out how it was important in the U.S. to compliment in a way that would be considered insincere flattery in his country. This was especially true when eating dinner in an American home. "At first I said only 'thank you'; I didn't mention the food, but I saw how the other Africans kept saying how 'delicious' the food was. I had to look the word up in a dictionary," he said.

While the American is taught from childhood that it is a sign of bad manners and ingratitude not to say 'thank you," in India these words are to be avoided, for "thank you" signifies finality and thus terminates rather than furthers the desired ongoing relationship. "Saying 'thank you' is like giving money in the market; it's just like a mere exchange which has ended," according to one Indian.

Displaying gratitude or praise after receiving a gift or favor is thus considered improper in many Asian countries, for any compliment directly to someone's face is suspected as being false. The speaker also runs the risk of not showing enough gratitude, thereby embarrassing the donor. The appropriate response is the indirect one; a grateful recipient should tell a third person, who will in turn transmit the message to the donor. This downplaying of the direct compliment can dishearten an American hostess, however, who feels that she has gone out of her way to prepare an especially pleasing dinner only to find her guests unappreciative – at least in American terms.

5. INDIVIDUALISM, FREEDOM, AND PRIVACY

Most visitors are struck by the amount of individual freedom in American society, the right of each person to, as it is currently expressed, "do his own thing." Some are deeply impressed; others are appalled. A Tanzanian, for example, had encountered "too much freedom" in terms of what he considered excessive individualism and thought this would be difficult to adjust to. An Indonesian agreed but felt that while this free, open style would be inappropriate in his homeland, it did suit the American culture.

While the American is willing to foresake a certain measure of efficiency and order for the sake of liberty, a Pole felt that this was misplacing priorities. "America has a lot of liberty — maybe too much — for you have many social problems. Liberty is used in the wrong way, as when certain groups use it against the government. All forces should go in the same direction to develop the country."

This is, of course, a mirror-image reversal of the pluralistic American notion, which features differing views and competing forces. A Brazilian compared the democratic process in the U.S. to a large sheet which was being pulled in all directions at once. Because the competing forces in the U.S. tended to cancel each other out, the sheet remained taut, that is, the governmental process remained viable. He added that this pattern would not work in many other societies, however, given the overriding power that one group or a few organizations held. The sheet would be pulled to one side; a government of competing factions would not stand.

Occasionally the point about "too much freedom" comes up in the context of the easy availability of handguns in the U.S. A Ghanaian had heard that "having a gun in the U.S. is like having a small pocket knife in Africa." A Vietnamese told of a cartoon that he had seen in his country of an American riding a bicycle with a firearm strapped across his back. A policeman stopped him and asked him if he had a license for his bicycle. Visitors in general find it incomprehensible that there are not tighter gun control laws.

Freedom is not without its defenders, however. A Senegalese was impressed by the right to speak freely as evidenced by the Watergate hearings. "We don't have a Watergate, but we don't have freedom of expression either," he said. "Everything is free," added a Zambian. "You can talk about the Watergate scandal any place. This is different from Zambia. If I said that I saw a minister and a girl in a dark corner, I would be dismissed without being given a reason." Particularly impressive to an Indonesian was the way one could oppose the government openly in the U.S.

It was not so much political as social freedom which caught the eye of a Honduran student. "You can do as you want as long as you don't hurt anybody else. I stay in a boys' dorm, but girls go in and out day and night. I'm not saying I'm against this," he was quick to add.

Coupled with the American's concept of individual liberty is the idea that he has a right to privacy, a term which, as we mentioned earlier, has no translation in several other languages. A Nepalese noticed that when an American was ill, others pretty much left him alone. That he seemed to prefer this isolation struck the Nepalese as strange. A Filipino added that in his society a person needed the constant presence of friends when he was sick to give him a sense of security and a sense that he was really loved.

Tied to this notion of privacy is a reluctance on the part of Americans to answer what they consider "personal" questions. "It is normal for us to ask about the life of a friend," said a Vietnamese, "but when I asked an American, 'How much is your salary?' he told me that Americans didn't discuss such things. I only wanted to make a comparison."

The tendency of Americans to go their own ways rather than seeking out their neighbors in hotels and boarding houses was disconcerting and somewhat eerie to several visitors, one of whom remarked that he hadn't seen a single person at his hotel. He had only heard footsteps going by his door.

The positive and negative sides of individualism were brought home to a Korean when he observed how Americans kept their private homes neat and clean but allowed public places to become untidy. A probing Filipino was still wrestling with a philosophical dilemma: "With the accent on individualism, how can Americans overcome an attitude of ennui or boredom? What are they living for?" he wondered.

6. SELF–RELIANCE AND THE NUCLEAR FAMILY

A Thai economist put his finger on what seemed a conflict in the way we ordered our society. He noticed a general sense of chaos in our family life and in particular a lack of discipline in raising children. Yet out in society, there seemed to be great discipline. People would queue up, accept responsibility, and in general things seemed well-ordered. How did we bring this order out of chaos?

What he viewed as disorderly upbringing, the American would term teaching the child to be self-reliant. Because they are constantly trying to avoid making the child too dependent on them, American parents never seem to have him completely in check. At the same time they are trying to instill a sense of responsibility. It is only through what appears to the outsider as abrasive interfamilial relationships that the American young person develops the sense of responsibility or discipline to function in the society at large.

This self-reliance was a positive trait to one Korean, who was trying to instill it in his own children. Yet a fellow countryman felt that despite certain benefits this system afforded the child, there was a neglect of his "existence" brought on by the need to quickly disentangle him from the protective web of the family.

"In the U.S. children have freedom to make their own decisions. In

Afghanistan, it is difficult for one under 15 years old to do so," commented another visitor, who added that marriage would be discussed with one's parents, and that traditionally in the village it was they who made the decision.

Many visitors tend to look with disfavor on the nuclear family, which they believe fails to engender the sense of warmth and interdependence afforded by the traditional extended family. A Czechoslovak was surprised at the "pick up and leave" attitude that Americans seemed to have, for at home before one would move or change position in life, he would consult at length with his family. It was a big undertaking "to leave one's home and garden."

It was a breakdown in traditional morality, according to a Jordanian, that led to unruly behavior among American young people. "In Jordan we tell a child what is right and wrong before he does anything. You let a child do anything and tell him only after he has done something wrong. Thus he is confused." A visitor from Dominica noted that American parents apparently did not believe in "spare the rod and spoil the child." In his visit to an American home, not once did he see any of the children get a spanking, even though they repeatedly disobeyed. Yet a Thai woman found that the nuclear family had certain distinct advantages: children developed self-confidence and a healthy sense of independence.

The do-it-yourself aspect of the self-reliant American family, particularly the male's acumen concerning household chores, came as a surprise to many. "In Viet Nam the wife must take care of everything around the house," said one visitor. "Seventy percent of the women don't work outside the home. In the U.S. the husband goes to the supermarket and knows about the prices. In Viet Nam the husband knows nothing about the family's needs." An Indonesian woman echoed her sentiments: "The American husband is willing to help his wife with the housework; this never happens in my country."

A Kenyan felt, however, that the American housewife was not respected and that a teenage girl would not look up to the housewife as a model to emulate. He contrasted this with the attitude in his country, where the role of housewife and mother was revered. Another negative factor was noted by a Sudanese woman, who attributed Americans' marital problems to the fact that husband and wife are separated so much of the time. "They only see each other after 5 o'clock and on weekends. The men are exhausted, and the women are worn out," she said.

The sudden need to be self-reliant can be somewhat disconcerting to the newly arrived. Following a visit to a local high school, a Filipino expressed surprise at the self-service style in the cafeteria: "We even had to bring our own trays back." Though a Korean visitor was getting used to his more independent existence, the need to do his own laundry and prepare his meals caused him to "really appreciate the value of my wife." A Tanzanian, on the other hand, appreciated certain aspects of the more self-reliant American approach. "In general, the American people are without bias. They leave a man on his own, to let him see both the good and the bad."

When traditional American self-reliance is interwoven with the social changes brought about by the Women's Liberation movement, many visitors are doubly confused. A Filipino, for example, was accustomed to the chivalrous approach of offering his bus seat to a woman. Since he was familiar with Women's Lib in the U.S., he now had to agonize over whether or not to get up whenever a woman stood near him on the bus. Finally he hit on a compromise. He got up, as if to go to the door, thereby making the seat available without actually offering it.

7. INFORMALITY AND MORALITY

Coming from societies which in the main stress neat, formal, and (by American standards) conservative clothing styles, many visitors are shocked by what they view as Americans' slovenly way of dress. Since many also come from countries where great attention is paid to consciously controlled bodily movements, the American's relaxed, slouching manner is often interpreted as crude and impolite. Conversely, the visitor's demeanor may appear rigid and stilted to the informal American. While the international visitor cannot understand how an American student can wear a T-shirt and jeans to class, the American will be dumbfounded when the visitor shows up for a picnic wearing a coat and tie.

"You can wear anything," said a Filipino. "In my country it looks funny for a man to wear high-heeled shoes or dirty short pants. People would say that he's loco."

A Thai doctor compared the orderliness of Americans in banks and cafeteria lines with the disorder in the way they dressed, especially in "a high place like the Capitol." Numerous visitors have noted the absence of regimentation in American high schools. "In our country students have to wear uniforms — like in the army," said a Korean. An Afghan was surprised by the "picnic-type, hippie-style" clothing worn by the students and by their lack of discipline. The classroom seemed to him more like a hotel or restaurant with three or four students seated around each table and the teacher wandering in and out.

Occasionally, however, visitors will comment favorably on the more informal American style. When an Indian complained that American youth were sloppy in dress and manners, a physician from Colombia countered that the bell-bottomed, barefoot look was a healthy sign of liberation. After listening to a Jamaican woman comment critically on the informal attire worn by American women to the Kennedy Center, a Ghanaian woman shot back: "Does that change their enjoyment of the music? These changes are part of the 20th century. It used to be that clothes excluded people from participating."

Part of the problem for many visitors is simply finding out how to fit in. They could live with American informality if only they knew what was expected in different social situations. "What is normalcy in the U.S.?" asked a Ghanaian woman, pointing out that there was no clear-cut pattern of proper conduct. "It is very difficult to say what is expected," she added. Perhaps the most helpful clue is simply to tell new arrivals to expect the unexpected in this freewheeling society in which change may well be the only constant.

The ambivalent attitude towards American informality was clearly illustrated in the comments of a Kenyan who was back for a second trip to the U.S. Initially he was shocked to see a high-level executive mingling with his underlings at a company baseball game. He later grew to see a positive side to this equalizing aspect of American life as epitomized by a university dean cheering wildly with his students at a Saturday football spectacular.

Some visitors find it hard to separate informality from immorality and, in fact, often tend to equate the two. Provocative clothing and public displays of affection lead to the conclusion that America is on the way to moral ruin. This suspicion is confirmed by the plethora of pornographic bookshops and topless nightclubs of the typical inner city.

"As an African traditionalist, I was shocked to see the neglect of Christian principles. We went to a night spot to drink beer and were surprised to see a naked woman dancing. Decency in dress seems to exist only among the elderly; the young people have forgotten it. Jeans are not bad, but they put on patches. You have advanced too much; the thinking is going down," concluded a Tanzanian.

Startling to a Ugandan was the way American girls went "nearly naked" on the street, and a Guatemalan agreed that girls "showed more than they should. Girls in my country wear miniskirts, but nothing like these."

It was anomalous to a Nigerian that the country which had sent so many missionaries abroad should be losing its religious fervor. A Korean was surprised by the widespread legal sale of pornography, and a Vietnamese was shocked by the embracing and kissing he had noticed while visiting a high school, pointing out that such conduct would not be tolerated in his country. "Ten or twelve years ago we were much stricter concerning young people kissing in the street," said a Spaniard, "but now we are following in your footsteps. You are the locomotive; we are the caboose."

Though Americans are sometimes perceived as not moralistic, they are invariably viewed as legalistic, as exemplified by the strict adherence to traffic rules and regulations. Numerous visitors have commented favorably, if at times patronizingly, on the orderly traffic pattern here as opposed to the highway chaos in their homelands. This salutary result in the U.S. is brought about, in their view, by a naive, almost childlike sense of obedience to the rule of law.

A Peruvian surgeon was surprised by the emphasis an American doctor would put on protecting himself from legal liability. "His action might be morally blameless, but he could still be responsible legally. I don't know of a single physician in Latin America who has liability insurance; he works only on moral responsibility," said the surgeon.

8. CRIME

If they know nothing else about Washington, D.C., and other major American cities, most visitors have undoubtedly heard about the high crime rate in the nation's capital and other metropolitan centers. Reports are brought back by fellow countrymen who have spent some time in the U.S., the stereotype of cities under criminal siege is implanted, and fear takes firm root in the visitor's psyche. Once he arrives in Washington, he is warned by well-meaning taxi drivers, hotel clerks, program officers, and just plain citizens to padlock his door, travel in groups, and go into hiding after dark. This fear for personal safety clearly precludes a satisfactory social life for someone who cannot be coaxed out of his hotel at night even by the assurance that door-to-door taxi service is available.

A Congressional Fellow from Pakistan could not fathom how such an "advanced society" could have a capital that was divided into "a safe and an unsafe zone." This division was dramatically illustrated for a Yugoslav woman by an American friend who laid a knife across a map of D.C. to indicate the area where it was safe to walk at night. Particularly distressing to a Guyanese was the way a visitor had to be announced at apartment buildings and the fact that all the rooms had heavy chain locks. A Korean was surprised by the metal grating across store fronts and the protective windows in post offices. "Americans have everything in terms of material goods but lack peace of mind. It seems that they live in tension and nervousness," he said. Violence in the U.S. grew out of the American accent on pragmatism, which tended to create a lack of morals, theorized a Nigerian.

This stereotype of lawlessness, though in part created by the current crime problem, has its roots for many visitors in the gangster and cowboy movies widely shown abroad. An occasional visitor will lump all these images together in his mind and expect to see in contemporary urban America a reenactment of the shoot'em-up heyday of Jesse James or Al Capone. "The people are very rough; it's a cowboy type of life. You have to confine yourself to your room and your studies," a Zambian was told before embarking for the U.S. He was greatly relieved to find the ruthless cowboy absent from the current American landscape.

Thus some visitors are surprised to find that the spectre of violence is not haunting their every footstep. The relative calm of life in D.C. encouraged a Nigerian, who had been told that "people would be shooting all the time." A Ghanaian thought all Americans would be brandishing pistols and was surprised to find that only policemen had them in evidence. "The society is not as violent as one was led to believe," added a Guyanese.

Our challenge at the International Center has been to try to allay the fears of the visitors and at the same time to caution them about the very real danger of crime — to strike in their minds some kind of balance between incapacitating dread and complete abandon. As discussed earlier, for many visitors the pendulum has already swung far in the direction of fear; we thus must often try to bring it back to a more realistic position. Achieving the vital balance between fear and frivolous unconcern so that the visitor can start his program in a confident, yet sufficiently cautious,

9. TIPPING, TAXES, AND "SALES"

Somewhat surprising has been the repeated criticism of tipping and the sales tax. To many visitors tipping appears to be giving something extra for what one is already paid to do, and the failure to include the sales tax in the stated price of an article is sometimes construed as a trap for the unwary. Africans have been particularly vocal in denouncing tipping, and a Tanzanian pointed out that his government had prohibited the practice as "an exploitation of visitors."

A Ghanaian felt it was demeaning to give small change to a man whom he perceived as almost begging for it. He would be glad, he said, to simply give the man some money as a gesture of goodwill; it was the ritualized aspect of tipping that seemed crass. How, asked a visitor from Malawi, could one show genuine appreciation for service rendered since the tip was more or less automatic? Several Ghanaians, after pointing out how the forced nature of tipping made them feel extremely uncomfortable, asked if Americans would excuse them if they did not tip since they were foreigners. Rather than excuse them, of course, the American service people would simply conclude that all Ghanaians were cheap.

"One of the disadvantages to living in the U.S. is giving the tip; it makes me feel uncomfortable. I always have to look up in a booklet how much to give," said a Vietnamese. "Why don't you pay proper salaries? Then you won't have to tip," added a Kenyan.

Unlike this gentleman, however, most visitors seem unaware that it is the expectation of income from tips that allows employers to set the base salary of service people at a low level. When the visitors learn that the tip is not really something "extra" but rather a necessity for the service person, they appear more willing to comply with this discomforting custom.

Equally perplexing to some visitors is the "hidden" sales tax. After picking out an article for $2.98, they sense that foul play is afoot when the cashier's sleight of hand suddenly brings the price to over three dollars. "It gives me a real headache," complained a Nigerian, who was slightly mollified when told that since there was no tax on drugs, the aspirin that he bought for his headache would escape the troublesome tax. We point out that actually there is an important political reason why the sales tax has traditionally been divorced from the rest of the price; in this way voters know exactly how much they are paying in taxes and can consider this factor when it comes time to elect their representatives.

A final suspicion-arousing aspect of American commercial practices is the repeated use of the word "sale." How, we are often asked, can one distinguish the genuine sale from the phony? Americans, of course, are also seeking such a talisman, so obviously no advice is foolproof. We suggest that they look for a "Regularly_____, Now_____" advertisement, which is more often an authentic sale than is an ad reading, "Comparable_____."

10. RACE RELATIONS

Comments from international visitors concerning the current racial situation in the U.S. mirror the confused, conflicting views expressed by Americans. Sharp attacks on lingering racial discrimination are mingled with expressions of surprise that race relations is not as big a problem as some visitors had been led to believe. While some complain of discrimination at the hands of white Americans, others are distressed that they are not more warmly received by the blacks. Many visitors find themselves flung, as it were, into a chess game already in progress. Unable to identify fully with either the white or black participants, they seek to feel securely at home in their new cultural milieu without becoming embroiled in the black/white confrontation. They want at once to participate in American society and yet to serve as spectators as our racial drama unfolds.

"Racial discrimination is the thing I don't like about the U.S.," said an Ethiopian student. "Asians have an easier time because their hair is straight and smooth, but the African's hair is kinky. Yet once white Americans find out that you are African rather than black American, the door is open.

"There is always a tension between blacks and whites here, and the situation seems to be getting worse. At the university I attend, black Americans have their own place to eat. If you see a white walking with a black, chances are the black is an African. I have gone out with a white girl, but black Americans tell me not to do so," he added.

A Chinese visitor, on the other hand, was surprised to see so many blacks going out with whites, for he had envisioned much more segregation than he had encountered. Similar sentiments were expressed by an Indian, who felt that the actual state of race relations gave lie to the negative stereotype he had brought from his homeland. "The black American holds his head high; he has a lot of dignity and freedom," he said.

"I used to think that at least in the South there was more segregation," added a Malawian student, who had found a far warmer reception in his southern university than he had ever expected. A visitor from Dominica was equally surprised to find that in the U.S. he was not the object of the dreaded "hate stare – where somebody looks at you like they want you to disappear."

Two Tunisians disagreed about the extent of integration in the U.S. One had found much more evidence of integration than he had expected and cited as an example the large number of racially mixed couples he had seen. Social pairing off of blacks and whites was not a true measure of actual integration, according to the other man, who maintained that there was still considerable segregation in other aspects of American life, such as housing patterns.

Africans sometimes feel that American blacks, whom they thought would welcome them as brothers, are giving them the cold shoulder. "People tend not to be bothered; there has been a poor response from the blacks," said a Tanzanian. "Black Americans don't help you," added a visitor from Zaire.

Part of the problem appears to be linguistic. The Malawian student in the South found it extremely difficult to understand the blacks' accent; they found it equally difficult to understand him. This inability to communicate effectively with American blacks had been particularly disappointing to a Nigerian, who never expected to find a language barrier between those speaking the same tongue. An Ethiopian could not make himself understood to a black waitress and was embarrassed by having to repeat his order several times. The reluctance of some Africans to initiate conversations, coupled with their clipped, unfamiliar accent, can also lead American blacks to conclude that the Africans are distant and haughty.

With all the problems bound up in the complex racial issue, the comments of a Chinese visitor brought a measure of temporary relief. Having heard about racial segregation in the U.S., he set out to hail a tax-cab. Black taxis whizzed by. White taxis passed in great numbers, and there were even a few black and white taxis. But very rarely was there a yellow cab, clearly the only type of taxi available for an Oriental passenger.

11. TEACHER-STUDENT RELATIONS

Perhaps nowhere does the informal, egalitarian American style come to life more forcefully for many visitors than in the classroom. Coming from cultures where the teacher is near the top of the social hierarchy, the visitors are stunned by the slouching, "disrespectful" demeanor of the students and the easy, often flippant interchange between the teacher and students in the U.S. In fact, it is often difficult for them to tell who the teacher is — so closely do his long hair and mod attire mirror the style of his outspoken charges.

Contrast this with the deferential respect accorded the teachers in many cultures, where the mere presence of the professor strikes a mixture of fear and awe in the obeisant students. No one would mistake the teacher for a student in such a setting, for he is so clearly the focal point, the center of ideas which radiate out to those who fall within his omnipresent aura.

Honorific titles such as *Sunsengnim* in Korean and *Aacaan* in Thai have no exact English equivalent, making it difficult for some new arrivals to refer to the teacher with the respect they feel he deserves. Casting about for an appellation of sufficient esteem, a Korean finally called an elementary school principal "Mister President." A Thai student told how she would snap smartly to attention as a sign of respect whenever one of her professors would pass by during her first few days at an American university. Much to her surprise and chagrin, the startled professor would rush over to ask her what was the matter. How could she possibly make her behavior understandable to someone unfamiliar with the whole cultural heritage which had conditioned her reflex display of respect? She soon learned that what was an indispensable show of courtesy in her culture was a confusing, meaningless gesture in the American milieu.

Though they are initially stunned by the easygoing banter between teacher and students, visitors often come to see a positive side to the participatory American pattern. "In our country, the teacher teaches, and the student accepts. I am impressed by the freedom to express which exists in American schools," said a Vietnamese.

"I was really shocked at first because there was no difference between teacher and students. We have been brought up to not speak until spoken to; we have been spoon-fed. In the U.S., the classroom is open, and one can criticize the teacher; he will admit it if the student can do something better. We may go out drinking with an American prof, but we respect him in the classroom," added an Ethiopian.

We have received conflicting comments as to whether the seminar format is a familiar one abroad. Younger visitors especially, from such countries as India, Indonesia, and Turkey, have insisted that there is now more questioning and exchange of opinions in the classroom and training seminar. Older visitors generally draw more of a distinction between the seminar style in the U.S. and the procedure at home. A Chinese pinpointed the differences nicely. "Participants in a seminar in China are encouraged to take an active part in the discussion, but it must be done at the proper time, that is, when the principal speaker is finished. The seminar is more formal there than in the U.S. There would not be the same give and take," he said.

A debate among several Turks concerning the relative merits of the school systems in the U.S. and Turkey reflects the basic ambivalence with which many visitors view the more pragmatic American course offerings as opposed to their own humanities-centered curricula. One Turk maintained that his system was superior, for it acquainted the students with more general knowledge of the world and thus made Turks better informed than Americans. Another Turk disagreed. "Your educational system is excellent because of its specialization. This is our problem in Turkey; this is why we are in the United States. We shouldn't just learn all about the world," he said.

12. LACK OF KNOWLEDGE ABOUT THEIR COUNTRIES

Particularly disheartening to many new arrivals is Americans' lack of knowledge of and interest in their countries and cultures. Having never heard of his country, several Americans asked an Ethiopian if he were from France. A midwestern farmer thought Egypt was somewhere near Georgia. Repeated pointless questions were driving an El Salvadoran to distraction. "They ask what kinds of houses we live in and if we drink Cokes; they seem to think we are still throwing spears," he said. An otherwise enjoyable evening with an American family was spoiled for a Thai when he was asked if there was cellophane (Scotch) tape in his country.

Equally distressing is the general absence of international news in the American press. A Costa Rican wanted to know why there was not even a *"triste noticia"* (the least bit of news) about Latin America, while newspapers in his country carried approximately 50 percent news concerning the U.S. Occasionally, however, a visitor will challenge the assumption that Americans are alone in their ignorance of the rest of the world. When a Kenyan mentioned that he had found it impossible to get international news on the radio except for constant references to Viet

Nam, a Nigerian countered: "Why should Americans be that interested in what happens in Africa? In fact, how many Kenyans are that interested in what happens in Nigeria?"

Because the average American on the street has not had much exposure to other cultures, he often assumes too much in speaking to foreigners when he gives complicated directions or refers to organizations or events that would require an American background to understand. When a Nigerian asked an American for directions to the nearest restaurant, the latter quickly replied: "Go straight for two blocks, turn to the left, then to the right, then back to the left." "Naturally we couldn't find the restaurant," said the Nigerian, adding that for someone like himself, who had previously traveled abroad, it was possible to get around on his own. For someone who had never before set foot outside his own country, however, he felt that instructions should be slower and clearer.

A confluence of geographical and psychological factors has apparently shaped the Americans' attitude toward the outside world. The mere fact of our longstanding isolation, coupled with our feeling of economic independence — only recently challenged — have tended to make us an inward-looking, basically self-sufficient people. Having secured a psychological divorce from Europe (the "Old World"), immigrants have long taken pride in becoming part of a "New World," in which to Americanize meant essentially to conform to a predominantly WASP model. Since the New World was clearly superior to the Old, what need was there to know about the countries beyond our ocean doors? Such a mentality has made it difficult for many Americans to have much interest in, let alone appreciation for, other nations and cultures.

Two world wars and two Asian conflicts have drawn us inexorably into the international arena. The Peace Corps has acquainted thousands of Americans with radically different ways of life, and the numerous departments of international studies at American universities have started others on the road to increased intercultural awareness. Inroads have been made, then, into traditional American isolationist views, but attitudes held for two centuries cannot be totally whisked away by the relatively recent move to a more international outlook. It is here that the international visitor clearly has an important role to play. For if he is willing to take the initiative, he can — by informing Americans about his country and culture — help bring about an end to the inane questions he is now often forced to field.

The obvious intent of this book was to show that it is unrealistic and injurious to satisfactory communication to assume that all peoples share the same basic assumptions, values, and attitudes. Pascal well summarized the actual situation when he pointed out that what was truth on one side of the Pyrenees was error on the other. The very notion of what is true, beautiful, and proper undergoes a striking metamorphosis as one crosses cultural boundaries. In concentrating on the differences, we hope to help dispel the simplistic scratch-the-skin-they're-all-the-same nostrum, which has tended to impede rather than facilitate intercultural communication. Barriers cannot be broken down if they go unnoticed, and without awareness of cultural differences, communication will either necessarily be at the most superficial level or will result in ships passing in the night if a more profound topic is broached.

While accentuating the differences, however, we would like to caution against going to an equally unserviceable position, reflected in some recent writings, which seems to maintain that unless one has the psychological insight of Freud, the compassion of Gandhi, and the patience of Job, intercultural communication is a hopeless undertaking. If this were true, the citizens of each country could simply become islands unto themselves, for there would be no hope of ultimate communication.

The challenge is to search out a middle ground between the "everybody's the same" and the "everybody's too different" camps, to be aware of cultural differences but to use this insight to further rather than inhibit intercultural communication. Several visitors have suggested ways of closing the cultural gap so as to derive the most rewarding experience possible from their stay in the U.S. An Indian woman told of the advice she gave her daughter-in-law on the eve of the latter's journey to the U.S. "Do not imitate them, for at best you will be a cheap product. Be a true Indian. Do not, however, hesitate to imbibe what is best in them; learn to discern, admire, and respect that which is noble in them. Ultimately you will find certain similarities, although we are not the same."

"To take the roses but not the thorns from the American way" was how the challenge was presented by a woman from the Philippines. An Ethiopian who had spent many years in the U.S. advised new arrivals to venture out and immerse themselves in American society as he had done. While it had its unpleasant moments, he felt that the educational experience was well worth it.

In the last analysis intercultural communication does involve a certain measure of risk, a plunging into the unknown, that is bound to have its share of emotional ups and downs. But the gain is great if one can penetrate, however imperfectly, into the thinking and customs of another culture. With this sense of adventure life then has a new, richer dimension. Chesterton boldly captured this spirit when he reminded us that man would never discover new oceans if he were afraid to lose sight of the shore.